PORTRAITS OF GENIUS

Portraits of Genius

BEATRICE SAUNDERS

John Murray

FIFTY ALBEMARLE STREET LONDON

© Beatrice Saunders 1959

Printed in Great Britain by
William Clowes and Sons, Limited, London and Beccles

Contents

Acknowledgements

The following illustrations are by courtesy of The National Portrait Gallery: facing pages 20, 46, 54, 68, 94, 116, 126, 138, 148; Radio Times Hulton Picture Library: facing pages 36, 168, 188, 200; The Marchesa Origo: facing page 158.

Introduction

THE aim of this book is twofold: first to sketch the lives and draw the portraits of these splendid authors, and secondly, to trace the course of genius. My first aim may seem unnecessary, but for some years I have been astonished that so little is known, by the average reader, of the lives and characters of these exceptional men. Friends tell me that they are interested, but have not the time to wade through a mass of letters, biographies and autobiographies. I have therefore tried to perform this task for them, in the hope that they will be tempted to explore further. I chose these particular authors because, without exception, I have derived immense pleasure from their writings, and in most cases I have admired them as men. To write of men for whom one has a profound admiration is so much easier than to write of men with whom one is not in sympathy.

With regard to my second aim—to trace the course of genius— this is of course an ambitious project, but it seems to me that that profound saying '*The surface of things is the heart of things*' is particularly appropriate here. If one attempted to delve too deeply into ancestry, heredity and environment, the mass of detail would almost certainly obscure the significant facts. Macaulay has said that 'Genius will find its own way, as it always has'. But I have been impressed also with the fact that the early circumstances and environment of a genius are very powerful influences on future development. We see, for instance, that four of my authors— George Fox, John Bunyan, William Cowper and Samuel Johnson —were profoundly influenced all their lives by the fear of eternal damnation, an obviously false doctrine taught in early childhood.

I have, in these essays, done my utmost to tell the truth, but it is obvious that the whole truth about these men will never be known. I have never approved of the deliberate 'debunking' of authors, for that is to write without mercy or tolerance. If, however, I have idealised these men, I must protest that love is a little blind; when we love someone dearly we unconsciously overlook many faults.

It may be said that some of these essays are not portraits, but sketches. May I plead, however, that as an artist I have discovered that a sketch will sometimes give a truer picture than a detailed portrait.

It may be said, also, that a diarist is not a genius, but in my opinion it is indeed a work of genius to write a really good diary.

BEATRICE SAUNDERS

Weybridge, May 1959

Montaigne

1533–1592

I T was in the year 1571 that a wealthy French lawyer, Michel de Montaigne, shut himself up in his painted room, high in a tower, in order to write in solitude. He was thirty-seven, but he had decided to retire from public affairs and to dedicate the remainder of his life to study and contemplation. Surrounded by old books—in his fine library he possessed a thousand volumes— he began to set down his thoughts and opinions, the thoughts which in time became the famous Essays.

Montaigne was neither melancholy nor mad, and he had always taken a keen delight in the company of his fellows. Indeed, he had been a courtier, a soldier and a magistrate, he had travelled extensively, he was acquainted with Kings and Princes, and he had loved beautiful women; but his health was uncertain and he realised that doctors could do little for him, so he had turned to Philosophy. 'I have seen the leaf, the blossom and the fruit. Now I see the withering', he said calmly. And if it seems strange that Montaigne should think of death when he was still in the prime of life, one must also remember the time in which he lived, one of the saddest and most dreary periods in the history of France, for the civil wars were raging, and men went in fear of their lives continually. The struggle between a dissolute clergy and a no less demoralised administration, between Medici and Guise, Valois and Bourbon, and Protestants and Catholics threatened almost to quench the light of civilisation in France. Men were burnt and hanged every day merely for their religious convictions, and Montaigne himself had often retired to bed expecting to be murdered before dawn. He was a Catholic, but one's own footman might be on the other side, and even brothers watched each other with narrowed eyes and secretly carried daggers up their sleeves.

Bands of robbers, too, roamed the countryside; they would strip a man and leave him naked, or beat him to death if he offered resistance. Twice in his life Montaigne fell into their hands and was saved only by a miracle. As for pestilences, they would sweep through the country like an evil wind, and before one could draw the curtains and shut out the horrid thing, whole families had perished. Few men lived past forty in those days and to die of old age was (as Montaigne said) 'a death rare, extraordinary and singular'. There were 'so many precipices of death'.

Every morning and evening, from the top of the tower in which he worked, a great bell would ring out the *Ave Maria*, a bell that shook the very walls and ceiling of his room, but Montaigne was not disturbed by this noise, for he was utterly absorbed in his task. He wrote and read continually, but not with any fixed plan. Virgil, Lucretius, Plato, Socrates, Cicero, Plutarch, Ovid, Horace; these were the writers he loved. They were his inspiration. Yet he had no ambition to emulate these brilliant men, and, unlike so many of his contemporaries, he had no desire for fame, or to be quoted in years to come. He declared that these Essays were merely 'the idle reveries . . . of a man in his nonage'. But he also confessed that he wished to leave behind for the benefit of his friends a record of his opinions and an intimate portrait of himself. 'Know thyself', said Socrates, whose philosophy Montaigne so deeply admired, and as Socrates had come to 'know himself', so was Montaigne determined to explore the mystery of his own soul and communicate that knowledge to the world. 'Whosoever shall so know himself let him boldly speak out.'

Reader, thou hast here an honest book [he said]. Had my intention been to seek the world's favour I should surely have adorned myself with borrowed beauties. I desire therein to be viewed as I appear in mine own genuine, simple and ordinary manner, without study or artifice, for it is myself I paint. My defects are therein to be read to the life, and my

2

MONTAIGNE

imperfections and my natural form, so far as public reverence hath permitted me.

Could anything be more honest? And yet, could anything be more sensible? The world of literature would be so much richer if more men had done this very thing.

It was winter when first Montaigne retired to his tower, but from his window he could see 'the golden summits of the hills of Perigord', and near at hand were the fields, streams, orchards and woods of his own estate, a peaceful and pleasant prospect. His painted room could hardly fail to inspire him, either, for on the beams of the ceiling the sayings of the great philosophers were engraved in Greek or Latin (it was the fashion of his time). These men were his gods, and he quoted from them continually. Their observations were the shining threads from which he wove the fine tapestry of his essays.

But let us glance at Montaigne as he stands beside us in that solitary tower. He is below middle height, thick-set and strong. He has, he tells us, a muddy complexion, and his humorous eyes are half hidden by drooping lids, yet his is a curiously attractive face. He wears silk stockings winter and summer, and has a weakness for wearing his father's old black cloak, he likes talking to sailors, carpenters and gypsies, is inclined to scratch his ears, never has his hair cut after dinner, detests the thought of poverty, loves to lie with his feet up, cannot sleep without a canopy and curtains, loves old shoes and old friends, dislikes the evening air, travels always with 'a handsome equipage', detests fogs, always carries a switch, and always wears gloves. He admits, too, that he likes comfort and luxury, hates smells and unpleasant sights, cannot endure the cry of an animal in pain, and dislikes business and discussions about money. Of one queer fad, also, he makes no secret—his servants are asked to wake him several times during the night simply because this interrupted sleep is the more delicious. (As a child his father had insisted that he should be wakened from sleep only by the sound of music, a spinet player being specially engaged for that purpose.)

But he also confesses to many 'short-comings'. He insists that he is 'idle, heavy and slow of understanding', he cannot make a speech without learning it word for word, he cannot remember names, or cast accounts, or saddle a horse, or fly a hawk, he cannot sing, or play on any musical instrument, nor does he excel at games or sports. Yet he admits, too, that he has never had a quarrel in his life and that his neighbours trust him, for they bring to him their money, jewels and private papers for safe keeping. It is strange, indeed, for while every other country house is guarded by soldiers he still employs only his old porter to stand at his gate.

Montaigne had inherited a fine chateau from his father, and here he received as guests many distinguished and learned men. From his well-kept orchards fruit was brought in abundance, grapes from his vineyard, wine from his great cellars. He had his fads, however, with regard to food. He disliked 'a confusion of meats and a clutter of dishes', he insisted on drinking from a very thin glass, and liked only his own particular servant to pour out his wine; he never drank wine neat, either, but always mixed with water.

Yet though good food was an excellent thing it was the company that counted. Witty and learned conversation was a delight, but 'wit above all'. 'Human understanding is marvellously enlightened by daily conversation with men', he said. He had noticed, too, that many interesting observations came from the lower end of the table. But most of all he liked to hear original views, especially those opposed to his own. When he was contradicted his attention was aroused at once, but never in anger.

> I advance to meet him who is contradicting me, who is interesting me . . . No hypotheses surprise me, no form of belief shocks me, however much opposed it may be to my own . . . In whatever hand I encounter the truth I greet it with joy and welcome it . . .

When the King of Navarre, with all his great suite, paid him a visit and slept in Montaigne's own bed, there was good company indeed, and to crown the visit Montaigne let loose a stag when the King departed, thus providing his Majesty with an exciting two days' chase. It was a great honour to have entertained a king, yet it gave one food for thought, for one realised that even he was not to be envied. He could not escape, for instance, fevers, gout and apoplexies any more than a peasant. And when old age 'hung heavy upon his shoulders', could his yeoman of the guard ease him of his burden? When he was 'astounded with the apprehension of death', could the gentlemen of his bed-chamber comfort and assure him? He might lie under a canopy of pearls and gold, yet this could not preserve him from a violent fit of the colic. It was clear, too, that cowardice, irresolution, ambition, spite and envy could agitate him as much as any other man. As for the pomp and luxury with which a king was sur-rounded, surely nothing could be so distasteful and clogging as abundance? What appetite would 'not be baffled to see three hun-dred women at its mercy, as the grand signor has in his seraglio'?

Montaigne had a positive veneration for wise and learned men, yet he had observed that even they sometimes lapsed into un-believable folly. Was it not plain that they followed each other blindly like sheep, that they set a high value upon worthless objects, that they were often profoundly unhappy when happiness lay within their reach? Was it not clear that they believed only what they wished to believe, and for as long as it pleased them to do so?

Montaigne's Essays were not published until he was forty-seven years old, but their success was undoubted, for his views threw an entirely new light on the prevailing manners and morals of the day. Here was a man of cool, impartial judgement who had the courage to tell the truth about himself and who could remain calm and moderate although surrounded by the most fanatical hostility. And was ever any author so frank and yet so wise? He was apparently interested in everything and had eyes for everything. Yet he made no attempt to teach or preach, he did not protest or flog himself to anger, nor did he throw up his hands in despair. He was, indeed, most human. 'If health and a fair day smile upon me I am a very good fellow; if a corn troubles my toe, I am sullen, out of humour, inaccessible.'

Even in the monasteries and nunneries his book found favour, although his essay 'Upon some verses of Virgil' was hardly suitable for the young and chaste. The nuns, therefore, cut out the offending pages before allowing the book to be read. But there were other criticisms; Montaigne was accused of impiety, materialism, licentiousness and epicureanism. He admitted, however, that he deliberately went out of his way to be frank on certain matters. 'I wish that this excessive licence of mine may draw men to freedom', he said. If his readers were offended then perhaps the fault lay in their own minds. 'I know very well', he added, 'that few will quarrel with the licence of my writings who have not more to quarrel with in the licence of their own thoughts.'

Alas, Montaigne did not live long to enjoy his fame, for at the age of fifty-five his health seriously declined. He was attended by eminent doctors, but he refused all their medicines. That they used such queer ingredients as the left foot of a tortoise, the liver of a mole, blood drawn from under the white wing of a pigeon, etc., seemed absurd; he would have none of them. He deplored, too, the frivolous reasons which doctors invariably gave to account for the death of a patient. They would say: 'But he lay with his arms out of bed' or 'He was disturbed by the rattling of a coach' or 'Somebody had set open the casement'.

Death, indeed, had no terrors for Montaigne; it was merely an interesting subject for speculation. It was a sober thought, of course, that a day would come when he would never again look out from his tower and contemplate the evening star, or ride behind his hounds, or buckle on his sword, or walk in his beautiful orchards. He wished to drink the cup of life to the last drop, 'to get drunk on it'. He felt sad, too, that there was no one into whose hands he could leave the management and use of all that he possessed. Unfortunately his wife and daughter had disappointed him and he had no son; he yearned for someone to cherish his old age and 'rock it to sleep'. Yet to die well; that was the great thing. He felt that it was 'no great matter to live', but it was important to meet death 'handsomely, wisely and firmly'. Indeed, in his opinion it was impossible to judge of a man's life until it was seen how he had met his death. As for himself, he hoped that death would find him at his usual occupations—planting his cabbages, or best of all, on horseback. He wanted no lamentations or farewells, either; it might be best that strangers should close his eyes.

But while life lasted, there was always beauty, and sleep (that can be full of dreams); there was red wine and white; there was solitude, and music, and old books; there was the nightingale singing at midnight and the dark sky brilliantly lit with stars. Above all, there was friendship—a glorious thing. He had had a great friend, M. La Boetie, a young fellow magistrate, to whom he had been devoted. Their affection had been 'the rarest and most wonderful thing, passing the love of brothers'. But La Boetie had succumbed to one of those mysterious fevers; he had been snuffed out like a candle. Montaigne could not think of his death without sadness.

Montaigne died at the age of fifty-nine, but neither planting his cabbages nor on horseback. He died in his bed, and it was a quinsy which put an end to his life. We are told that Mass was celebrated in his bed-chamber, and we can well believe that he died peacefully.

But his book remains, a perpetual delight. It is a book to saunter through, so that one can linger here and there, to ponder on his views. For whether we want his views on Friendship, or Sleep, or Glory, or Liberty, or Cowardice, or Anger, or Repentance, or Cannibals, or Fear, or Ancient Customs, or the Education of Children, it is all there. And we feel that Montaigne did not realise what fine things he had said until the words appeared on his manuscript.

It is true that these opinions do not resolve themselves into a philosophy, a design for living, and those who seek for his message will be disappointed. Indeed, we see that although Montaigne had pondered deeply on the ways of men and was himself such a master of the art of living, he could find no answer to that great riddle, that fascinating mystery. 'Que scais je?' he says—'What do I know?' Yet he succeeded with incredible skill in telling the truth about himself—a most difficult task. ''Tis a rugged path', he said, 'more so than it seems, to follow a path so rambling and uncertain, as that of the soul, to penetrate the dark profundities of its intricate internal windings. . . .'

In listening to Montaigne, also, we forget the vexations of the day. He had the rare gift of being willing and able to share himself with others, to take us into his intimate confidence, and bring us into his charmed circle. This country squire, who might have played a great part in politics or public life, preferred to sit in the solitude of his tower writing essays. But it is we who have gained. Governments may come and go, kings may lose their crowns and their heads, but human nature will still remain the most fascinating study on earth. Here is a delightful man, wise, scholarly, honourable, shrewd, witty and tolerant. He is no saint, or prig, or canting hypocrite; he is intensely human, and although as an author he has been described as a charming dilettante yet Shakespeare and Bacon were not ashamed to borrow from him. As for Madame de Sevigne, she declared that he was 'capital company'. 'Mon Dieu, how full is that book of good sense', she said.

Sir Walter Raleigh

1552–1618

IN pondering on the Elizabethan era—and there is certainly no more delightful occupation—we are convinced of one fact, that this age shines like a jewel in the history of England, and if by some devastating earthquake all other records were lost and yet this one jewel remained, we should still be rich, for never in any age was there such a vast outpouring of genius. Whether they were scholars, craftsmen, actors, writers, musicians or courtiers, the Elizabethans were immensely in love with life, and this tremendous enthusiasm was able to express itself with the greatest possible freedom and vigour. The English virtues, too —idealism, the love of liberty, beauty, nature and domesticity— were an integral part of the Elizabethans, and men were not ashamed to acknowledge such sentiments.

There was, however, another side to this fine picture, for where there is so much zest for life there is also brutality and lust for power, and if men are ambitious there is also bribery and corruption and treachery. A man's head was never safe on his shoulders for long, and many men died mysteriously from poisoning. As for the fate of traitors, that was ever before one's eyes. A man found guilty of treason was dragged through the city and hanged, drawn and quartered. Life was short and full of hazards. So with death just round the corner, heaven and hell were very real. Heaven was a shining city paved with gold and set with gates of pearl, and hell was so near that one could almost hear the crackling of the subterranean fires on a quiet night.

Into this fantastic world came Sir Walter Raleigh, a typical Elizabethan; one cannot possibly imagine him in any other setting. He was a handsome, bold, fascinating and brilliant man, six feet tall, with dark hair, curling beard and steel grey eyes. He dressed gorgeously, even for his day, in silk, satin, gold and silver. His ruffs were of beautiful Flemish lace, his boots of perfumed Spanish leather, and he wore magnificent pearls and jewels. He was the possessor, also, of the most plausible tongue. But whether or not he did actually spread his cloak in the mud for the Queen to walk on, is uncertain. Yet what was a cloak compared with the notice of a great and powerful Queen? It was the age of splendid gestures.

It is plain, however, that Raleigh did not become the Queen's favourite simply through one splendid gesture; there was far more to it than that. For the shrewd Elizabeth soon discovered that Raleigh was a man of vast ability. He had proved himself an accomplished soldier, but he was also a brilliant sailor and navigator, and his great ambition was to sail the seven seas and bring back for his Queen the glittering treasures which he knew were to be found. He declared that he could bring fabulous gold from the Indies, but by a better and shorter route than that used by the successful Spaniards. He was ruthless, fearless, resourceful, incredibly ambitious, immensely versatile, and panting for adventure. Nothing would deter such a man and no project seemed too difficult for him to attempt. He did realise, however, that he must go warily. One day, therefore, as he was standing in a window recess he glanced up at the Queen and wrote with the point of a diamond on one of the panes:

Fain would I climb but that I fear to fall.

She read it with a smile, and then, with her own hand, pencilled beneath:

If thy heart fail thee do not climb at all.

Here was a challenge, indeed, and Raleigh accepted it, for no climber was ever more bold or successful, and within three years of receiving the Queen's commission as an Army Captain he was knighted and superbly installed in the riverside palace

Sr WALTER RALEGH

SIR WALTER RALEIGH
by Houbraken

of Durham House in the Strand. His retinue consisted of forty persons (with as many horses) in magnificent liveries, the expenses of this gorgeous establishment being met by certain leases and patents granted by the Queen. A little later he was given most of the confiscated lands of the Desmonds in Munster; he was made Lord Warden of the Stannaries, Vice Admiral of the West, and eventually Captain of the Queen's Guard. When finally he was granted land in five English counties he had become one of the most powerful men in England.

This was Raleigh, a bold and glib adventurer, as he talked and swaggered through the glorious halls of Elizabeth's glittering Court, and when the light flashed on his brilliant jewels, many a man cursed him under his breath for a knave and an upstart. He was insolent, domineering and difficult, and as he had never been trained in a noble household he did not possess the tact of an experienced courtier. It is true that he came of an aristocratic family, but as a young man he had lived poorly in Devonshire, and apparently his three years at Oxford had not produced the requisite polish. He realised, however, that he could please the Queen, and there can be little doubt that he believed himself to be capable of ruling England, for men of far less capacity had aspired to that position.

In the meantime, his activities were ceaseless. He was an active Member of Parliament, he designed and built splendid ships, he helped to plan the fortifications at Portsmouth, and on his Irish estates he was continually planting, mining, draining, building and disforesting. He also wrote assiduously—books on trade, Parliaments, maxims of State, etc. But his greatest enterprises were connected with ships, and his privateers were constantly scouring every sea. He was determined that England should continue to hold the unchallenged domination of the New World. Colonisation was his dream and his passion. But the cost of his expeditions—financed by himself—was enormous; he was therefore continually importuning the Queen for anything that was to be given away. 'When will you cease to be a beggar, Raleigh?' she asked him one day. 'When, madam, you cease to be a benefactress', was the cool reply. He never, in fact, failed to claim, and receive, a reward for any service, however small. His post as Captain of the Queen's Guard also gave him opportunities of asking favours for friends, for which he exacted large sums.

This, then, is the picture we conjure up of Raleigh, but it is not by any means the whole of this extraordinary man, for the high imaginativeness which produced his fine political conceptions also gave him a taste for the arts, and he could produce some exquisite poetry. Spenser called him 'the summer's nightingale':

> Give me my scallop-shell of quiet,
> My staff of faith to walk upon,
> My scrip of joy, immortal diet,
> My bottle of salvation,
> My gown of glory, hope's true gage,
> And thus I'll take my pilgrimage.

Could anything be more felicitous than this? It is clear, in fact, that Raleigh, with all his worldliness, was very human, for he fell deeply in love with one of the Queen's Maids of Honour. But it is also clear that he pushed his cool self-confidence too far, for he knew that the Queen regarded it as a personal insult if any of her courtiers married without her consent, and when she asked, in a blaze of fury, whether there was any truth in the rumour of his attachment to Elizabeth Throgmorton, he lied unashamedly. 'I protest before God, ther is none on the face of the yearth that I would be fastened onto', he said. Yet he was probably already married, and on his return to London he was arrested and sent to the Tower, the poor Maid of Honour being also in sad disgrace.

It has been said that 'He who rises like a rocket will fall like a stick', and so it was with Raleigh. His rise to power had been meteoric, and his fall was great indeed.

> Stone walls do not a prison make
> Nor iron bars a cage

he wrote. But was he not whistling to keep up his courage? His was not the calm, contemplative temperament, and inaction was death to him.

Fortunately, before his disgrace, Raleigh had obtained, by much intrigue and importunity, the fine estate of Sherborne, in Dorsetshire, and here with his wife—to whom he was sincerely attached—he was allowed to spend his banishment. He had been released from prison but was debarred from Court—a most serious punishment, for without the Queen's friendship he was a beggar; she alone could dispense the favours which were essential to his plans.

As we follow Raleigh's career, in fact, we feel that few men have been so unfortunate, for when finally he persuaded the Queen to allow him to make an expedition to Guiana (that 'mysterious virgin land of gold') he was pursued by the most evil luck. He and his men suffered terrible hardships, they had to contend with devastating fever, floods, shortage of water, alligators and wild beasts. The expedition had cost him his whole resources, but the gold had not materialised. It was a tragedy. 'I am returned a beggar and withered', he said miserably, for he had hoped, if the expedition had been successful, that the Queen would have ended his banishment.

The Queen did not send for him, in fact, until his banishment had lasted for five long years, and until he had proved himself again by the part he took in the successful action (for which he was chiefly responsible) against Cadiz. This rich port was taken and burnt, the great Spanish fleet of ships was destroyed and all the rich merchandise captured. Raleigh had been in command of a squadron of twenty-two ships.

So Raleigh was once again Captain of the Guard. Once more he wore the splendid uniform and silver armour, and had the entrée to the Privy Chamber. Indeed, when his rival, the Earl of Essex, was tried for treason, Raleigh's hopes rose very high. He was called to give evidence against Essex, but the young Earl said scornfully, 'What booteth it to swear this fox?'

Raleigh's star, in fact, sank swiftly after the death of Essex, for the Queen was an old woman; she had no eyes for Raleigh;

she had loved the young Earl, and his death was a mortal blow to her. Raleigh was merely a clever tool which she had used for her own purposes. No, there was nothing more forthcoming from that direction. And when the Queen died, and Raleigh brazenly courted the new King, he met with no success. James did not like this bold adventurer, and his offer to raise a thousand men with which to fight Spain was coldly refused.

And then, almost without warning, the blow fell. The rumour flew round the Court that there was a plot against the King, in which Raleigh was implicated. It was treason, the most heinous of all crimes. So to the Tower again Raleigh was marched, and this time in such utter despair that he attempted (unsuccessfully) to commit suicide.

The trial of Raleigh took place at Winchester, and the mob cursed and threatened him savagely as he drove there. But what a mockery of a trial it was! 'Thou traitor' and 'Thou viper' hissed the prosecuting counsel (Coke) across the Court. And when Raleigh said, 'Let me answer; it concerns my life', Coke shouted, 'Thou shalt not'. The result of the trial, in fact, seemed a foregone conclusion, for although Raleigh defended himself eloquently—when he got the chance—and denied that he had ever plotted against the King, it was common knowledge that Raleigh belonged to the party in England which before Elizabeth's death was opposed to Scottish domination, a fact that was seriously against him. Therefore, with others, he was condemned to die.

And now, casting aside all pride and dignity, Raleigh begged frantically for his life. 'Save me, therefore, most merciful prince', he wrote, and signed himself 'Your penitent vassall'. He was certain that he would lose his head, and the thought of death was insupportable.

That Raleigh was reprieved on the scaffold is a piece of dramatic history, but he was sent back to the Tower, all his offices were forfeited, his Sherborne estate was stripped and rifled, he lost his plate, and debtors made heavy claims against him. Only, in fact, by the intervention of Cecil was a small part of his estate eventually saved.

Raleigh was allowed the use of the terrace for exercise, and here, dressed in a rich gown and trunk-hose, he would saunter up and down to show himself to the crowds on the wharf, who came from far and near to see him. Prince Henry, too, came to visit the unhappy prisoner, and was utterly fascinated by Raleigh's wonderful mind and schemes. The Prince, in fact, constantly begged the King to release Raleigh. But his royal friendship did the prisoner no good; it merely raised suspicion, and when finally the young Prince died, it was wickedly rumoured that Raleigh had poisoned him with a home-made cordial which the Queen had sent for when the Prince was expiring.

In the meantime, Raleigh wrote to everyone begging for favours, and no sooner was one favour granted by the King than the begging started again. Raleigh complained that the confinement was killing him, that he was in danger of death from 'the palsy' and of 'nightly suffocation by wasted and obstructed lungs'. He feared, indeed, that he was doomed, like so many prisoners, to die in the Tower, broken in mind and spirit. He would be buried under a stone in that grim citadel, where the walls were ten feet thick and the rats scuttled across the floors with evil intent. Never again would he sail across the great blue ocean on a fine ship, and land on a golden shore, where the palm trees waved and beckoned. Oh God, what anguish it was to be caught like this in a net, while lands containing fabulous wealth remained unexplored!

The longed-for release, however, came at last, and Raleigh stepped out of his prison. But he was, alas, prematurely old, lined and white-haired. That fertile brain, however, had already planned a large expedition in search of gold, and the King had been persuaded by his ministers to grant him a commission to make the voyage, with full power to command, and to take such arms as might be necessary for defence, the King reserving for himself one-fifth of all bullion and jewels found. James had insisted, however, on a detailed statement of the exact strength of the proposed expedition, with its objects, and destination, which 'on the word of a king' he promised to keep 'secret'.

Raleigh had invested in this enterprise every farthing that he could raise or borrow, and finally, in July 1617 he sailed, with fourteen ships in all, and about nine hundred men. He did not know, of course, that several secret agents sailed with him. He did realise, however—and so probably did James—that he might have to fight, and that if so it would be the Spaniards.

He sailed away with the highest hopes, but the expedition was a complete failure, for many men became ill and died, Raleigh himself was seriously ill with fever, one of his best captains committed suicide, and the crews eventually lost faith in Raleigh and became angry and discontented. There was also a scrap with the Spaniards, but it was not a serious affair, and Raleigh declared that the Spaniards were the aggressors. The great tragedy, however, was that Raleigh's son was killed and no real treasure was found. Raleigh returned home broken-hearted. 'What shall become of me now I know not', he said. 'I am unpardoned in England and my poor estate consumed, and whether any other prince or state will give me bread I know not.' To his wife he had to send the tragic news of his failure and the death of their first-born. 'I was lothe to write', he said, 'because I knew not how to comfort you; and God knows I never knew what sorrow meant till nowe . . . Comfort your heart, dearest Besse, I shall sorrow for us both.' And he added, 'My braynes are broken.' He was, in fact, utterly worn out, having barely slept during the voyage, but the real tragedy was that he had failed because the Spaniards had been forewarned of all his movements, and it was the King who was to blame; he had shown the Spanish Ambassador Raleigh's secret letter in which he had set out the exact number of ships and men, and the precise spot where the gold mine was supposed to be. King James had also assured the Spanish Ambassador that if Raleigh dared to attack or plunder any subjects of Spain he would be handed over on his return, to be hanged in Madrid.

Thus was Raleigh betrayed, and the Spanish Ambassador declared that all England should not save such a man from the gallows. Raleigh, in the meantime, was under arrest at Plymouth, where, knowing that he had been betrayed, he tried to escape in a boat, but was caught, arrested, and eventually sent to the Tower.

And now came the climax, for every subterfuge to prove Raleigh guilty of treason was unsuccessfully tried, so finally it was decided to issue a warrant for the death sentence of 1603 to be carried out, and on 24th October Raleigh was taken from the Tower and examined by the Council. He was told of his crime, warned that he must die, and from that moment was guarded night and day, to prevent him from committing suicide. A few days later he was taken to the King's Bench and sentenced to death. He was not allowed to say a word in his own defence and was conveyed to the gate-house prison.

The night before the execution Raleigh's wife was allowed to take a last leave of him, and at midnight they clung together and wept their last sad farewells. Through the rest of the night Raleigh wrote out the speech he intended to make on the scaffold.

The execution had been arranged for the early morning, before the people were astir, as it was Lord Mayor's day and all the citizens would flock to see the show. On the morning of 29th October, 1618, therefore, Raleigh was led to the scaffold. He wore a black velvet gown over a brown satin doublet, a ruff band, black taffety slashed breeches and ash-coloured stockings. He was surrounded by sixty guards, and in spite of the hour a crowd had assembled. He spoke for three-quarters of an hour, chiefly to explain the purpose of his expedition, but it was clear that he was weak and ill and could barely stand. 'I have a long journey to go', he said, as he put off his gown and doublet. Then he asked the headsman to let him see and feel the axe. 'Dost thou think I am afraid of it?' he said; then, as he handed it back, 'It is a sharp medicine, but it is a sound cure for all diseases.' When he was told how to kneel he said, 'If the heart be right it is no matter which way the head lies.' Then, 'Farewell, my lords', he said cheerfully, to a group of friends, as he embraced them, one by one. He was, in fact, extremely brave.

As for Raleigh's poor wife, she wrote to her brother asking to be allowed to 'berri the worthi boddi of my nobell hosben,

Sur Walter Raleigh, in your chorche at Beddington . . . God hold me in my wites', she added. But for some reason—not known—the body was buried in the chancel of St Margaret's, Westminster.

Our last glimpse of Raleigh, therefore, is of this once great man, waiting for death in his lonely cell. He is writing his last speech, and also a poem (found in his Bible after his death):

> Even such is time, that takes in trust
> Our youth, our joys, our all we have,
> And pays us but with earth and dust;
> Who in the dark and silent grave,
> When we have wandered all our ways,
> Shuts up the story of our days.
> But from the earth, that grave and dust
> My God shall raise me up, I trust.

The sad voice comes to us through the barred window, and we realise that he is trying to soothe himself with the thought that there is, after all, a higher life than that of the courtier.

Raleigh became after death far more popular than he had ever been in life, and it was said of him:

> Hee living was beloved of none,
> Yet in his death all did him moane,

But the reason is not far to seek, for Englishmen have always loved justice, and to Raleigh justice was shamefully denied. His trial is one of the most disgraceful in the history of English jurisprudence. Raleigh was neither honourable nor high principled, yet he was typical of the age in which he lived. His great abilities created great ambitions, and like Lucifer he fell.

So what shall we say of Raleigh? That he was a great Englishman, courageous, far-sighted, a fine pioneer and a good sailor. His love of England and his faith in her destiny brought out all the marvellous qualities of his mind—the wonderful initiative and power of imagination. He was, of course, greedy, unprincipled and rapacious, yet he spent his own fortune lavishly on his great patriotic schemes of colonisation. He failed because with all his vast ability he had not that quality of leadership which would have enabled him to change reverse into victory. At the moment of failure, for instance, during his last voyage, he could only blame and lament, with the result that his men fell away from him and he returned home a prisoner in his own cabin. He was, it is plain, too old and too broken by imprisonment to have undertaken such an expedition at that time.

Yet his works remain—a handful of beautiful poems, and his *History of the World*, probably the greatest work ever produced in captivity. Written in splendid style, it remains, although unfinished, a fine fragment conceived by a great mind. King James thought it 'too saucy in censuring the acts of Princes'. And that, perhaps, explains the whole tragedy of Raleigh's life and death; he sadly lacked diplomacy.

Sir Francis Bacon

1561–1626

WHEN we think of Sir Francis Bacon we picture him, magnificently dressed—for he loved fine clothes—moving with great dignity and a tremendous sense of his own importance through long galleries, royal state rooms and in the Law Courts. We see him walking in his own spacious gardens, or dining in almost royal state. We are told that on his marriage he was 'clad from top to toe in purple' and bought 'such store of raiments of cloth-of-silver and gold that he drew deep into his wife's portion'. That is the sort of man he was. But we see him, too, poring over his books, writing—for ever writing. He was a great scholar with a marvellous mind; as lawyer, scientist, philosopher, historian and essayist he stands out boldly and brilliantly—though without honour—in the historical pageant.

But he has summed up his own life so well that we cannot do better than quote from one of his essays:

> The rising unto place is laborious, and by pains men come to greater pains; and it is sometimes base, and by indignities men come to dignities. The standing is slippery, and the regress is either a downfall, or at least an eclipse, which is a melancholy thing.

Bacon's rising into place was indeed laborious, the standing was extremely slippery, and his downfall was truly 'a melancholy thing'. By industry, cunning and treachery he finally rose to 'great place' but he added little to England's prestige at the time. Yet he has left behind a collection of essays so wise, profound and attractive that we are bound to be grateful to him. And what is perhaps more, his name is inseparably connected with the great intellectual revolution which followed. He was not the inventor of the 'inductive method of science', but with his great comprehension and wonderful powers of observation he taught that all the arts were interrelated; he demonstrated how to generalise, how to link up significant facts and so produce a new theory. This brilliant English philosopher, in fact, created an immortal epoch in the history of science, which in time influenced the whole of the civilised world.

Bacon was the younger son of Sir Nicholas Bacon, Lord Keeper of the Privy Seal, and as a child he had been taken to Court to kiss the Queen's hand. Elizabeth had also visited his father's stately country house, Gorhambury, in Hertfordshire. No child could fail to be impressed by such a visit, for suddenly trumpeters had arrived at the gates, and the fantastic cavalcade had streamed into the park—horses and coaches, outriders, servants, attendants, courtiers and ladies, all in the most gorgeous attire.

Francis, as the son of the house, was brought forward to kneel before the Queen, and she was so impressed with his boyish dignity that she called him her 'young Lord Keeper', a remark that could hardly fail to stir the fire of ambition in such a precocious child.

Bacon, therefore, started with every advantage, and after three years spent at Cambridge he went to Paris, at the age of fifteen, with the suite of the English Ambassador. Here he wrote those *Notes on the State of Europe* which were published later. But it was at this time, too, that all his 'court hopes' were shattered, by the death of his father—a serious blow for such an ambitious youth, as all 'preferment' in Elizabeth's Court went by favour.

However, in the Parliament which was called in the year 1593 Bacon sat as member for the County of Middlesex, and he soon attained eminence as a debater. He was described by Ben Jonson as 'a noble speaker' and he was extremely well-read in history and literature. He did, however, cause great offence to the Queen by saying in Parliament that 'the English are not to be subject, base or taxable'. And this, of course, was the reason why his frequent appeals to the Queen for a post were met with chilling silence or polite refusal.

In the meantime, Bacon had acquired expensive tastes. He had a fine house and many servants. He loved wealth, precedence, titles, beautiful gardens, rich manors, curious cabinets, fine plate. For these he was prepared to stoop low, to fawn, to scheme, to work. But as a younger son his income was not a large one and he was already in debt.

It was at this time that he saw his opportunity, and began to cultivate the friendship of the Earl of Essex, that handsome, impulsive young courtier who was now swiftly rising to power through the favour of the Queen. Bacon, as a trained lawyer, was able to advise and assist with the drafting of State papers, etc., and in return Essex put his friend's requests earnestly before the Queen. When the post of Attorney-General became vacant Essex strongly urged the Queen to give it to Bacon, but it was finally bestowed elsewhere. Then for two and a half years Essex tried to secure the post of Solicitor-General for his friend, but again without success. 'Master Bacon', he said, 'the Queen hath denied me yon place for you and hath placed another . . . you fare ill because you have chosen me for your mean and dependence . . . I die if I do not somewhat towards your fortune; you shall not deny to accept a piece of land which I will bestow upon you.' Bacon demurred, but he soon accepted, and was presented with a property which he later sold for £1,800 (worth at least £20,000 to-day).

Francis's old mother, Lady Bacon, was well aware of her son's bitter frustration. 'I am sorry your brother with inward secret grief hindereth himself', she wrote to her other son. 'Everybody saith he looketh thin and pale.' But she did not like his friends, those expensive young men who lived in his house. She called them 'filthy, wasteful knaves, cormorant seducers' and 'instruments of Satan'. And very probably she was right.

Meanwhile, the friendship between Bacon and Essex grew and flourished, and Bacon always assisted with the splendid entertain-

SIR FRANCIS BACON
From the painting by Paul van Somer

ments given by his friend. But Bacon had time, also, for his
literary work, and in 1597 he published a book of essays, a work
that was obviously influenced by Montaigne's book (published
some nine years previously), yet it had its own particular charm,
and was very popular, being reprinted in a few months and
translated into Latin, French and Italian. It established his
reputation.

The fall and trial of the Earl of Essex stirred all England, but
his greatest friend, the cold and calculating Francis Bacon,
apparently decided that the fall of this powerful man would
probably mean the rise of another. When, therefore, he was
asked to put the case for the Crown against Essex he did not
refuse, and with icy deliberation he prepared the evidence.

All history knows how brilliantly and cunningly he did in
fact present his case, firmly brushing aside the excuses and
subterfuges of the prisoner. He declared that 'there was never
any traitor heard of but he always coloured his practices with
some plausible pretence'. And so Essex, his benefactor and one-
time friend, went to the block. 'Lord, be merciful to thy prostrate
servant', cried the prisoner, as the axe was about to fall. Was
there any pity in the heart of Francis Bacon as he saw the head
severed from the fair young neck? It is unlikely. The Queen paid
Bacon £1,200 for his services, and although many denounced
him as a traitor and even threatened his life, he had his answer.
'I thank God I have the coat of a good conscience', he said.

After Elizabeth's death Bacon lost no time in insinuating himself into the favour of the new King. He knew—none better—
how to flatter, how to agree with all that a King desired. When
someone hinted to him that it was time to look about him he
replied, 'Sir, I do not look about me; I look above me.' And his
rewards came very soon. After his long 'rising into place' and
many 'indignities' the laurels arrived. He was knighted in 1603,
he became Solicitor-General in 1607, a Privy Councillor in 1616
and Keeper of the Privy Seal the following year. In 1618 he was
made Lord Chancellor, and the same year raised to the Peerage
as Lord Verulam. He had now a very large income, and the pomp

and state in which he lived exceeded anything which had gone before. Three of his servants kept their coaches and some kept race horses. He gave himself regal airs, and if any Privy Councillors sat too near him he would icily bid them 'know their distance'. It was he, in fact, who governed England during the King's absence.

But the day of reckoning was near, for about a year later the Commons criticised the state of the Courts of Justice, and Bacon was charged with accepting bribes. He immediately appealed to the King and suggested cunningly that 'those that will strike at your Chancellor, it is much to be feared will strike at your Crown'. But the King could not save him; the guilt was too clear. And Bacon had no real defence; he was the ablest man in Europe and knew the law from A to Z.

He was forced to admit, with slight reservations, the charges brought against him, though at the same time he tried to blacken those who had accused him. But finally he threw himself on the mercy of his Peers. 'I beseech Your Lordships to be merciful to a broken reed', he implored. No man had ever had a fairer trial.

Bacon was condemned to pay a fine of £40,000, to be imprisoned in the Tower during the King's pleasure, and declared incapable of holding any office in the State or from sitting in Parliament. He was also banished from Court for life. But finally the sentence was remitted by royal order and he was released from the Tower, though he was never again allowed to sit in Parliament.

For a time Bacon refused to see anyone, and apparently he neither expected nor wished to survive his shame and misery. He begged his servants to leave him and to forget that he had ever existed. But when he had recovered a little he began to think again of his purse. 'I will not', he said, 'be stripped of my feathers.' And he still kept up a princely retinue. Then, although he was old, melancholy, loaded with debt and debarred from public life, he resumed his literary work. He turned to the intellectual pursuits he had always loved, and within five months of his retirement he had completed his *History of Henry VII*, started

24

his *History of Henry VIII*, sketched out his *History of Great Britain*, made notes for his *Digest of the Laws of England and Scotland* and prepared his *Dialogue on the Sacred War*. Other books appeared during the next few years, in spite of the fact that his health was rapidly declining.

Bacon's death was really the result of a scientific experiment, for he wished to find out whether cold would preserve food; therefore, one winter's day he descended from his carriage, bought a fowl, killed it, and with his own hands stuffed it with snow. During this operation he became very chilled, and was carried to the house of Lord Arundel, where a week later he died.

It is doubtful whether anyone really lamented his death, for his wife had become estranged from him, and in his thirst for fame he had violated the most sacred obligations of friendship and gratitude. There can be no doubt, either, that he had persecuted the innocent, tortured prisoners, plundered suitors and tried to pervert the course of justice with judges. He was a dangerous man with a corrupt mind. He had consented to the death of Raleigh, one of the greatest men of his time, he had deserted his own friend, Attorney-General Yelverton—when the latter was tried on some slight charge—and he had betrayed Essex. William Harvey has said that Bacon's eye was 'like the eye of a viper' and Pope has described him as the 'wisest, brightest, meanest of mankind'. But there can be little doubt, too, that in spite of his grandeur he was an unhappy man. He wrote:

> The World's a bubble and the life of man
>   Less than a span;
> In his conception wretched, from the wombe
>   So to the tombe;
> Curst from his cradle, and brought up to yeares
>   With cares and feares.
> Who then to frail mortality shall trust
> But limmes in water and but writes in dust. . . .

He left debts of £22,000, and it is unlikely that they were ever paid.

And so there remain his books, the histories, the philosophical treatises and the Essays. The essays, of course, are a great treasure, for from the very first sentence we realise that here is a brilliant intellect. The sentiments are too worldly and too cynical, yet here is profound wisdom and pregnancy of thought. Here, too, is an example of magnificent writing, with a superb economy of words. And, knowing his life, we can see how the pattern of it had moulded his very outlook. 'The most frequent of external causes,' he says, 'is that the folly of one man is the fortune of another.' What a strange statement! But he was speaking, of course, from experience. One can be quite certain that Bacon had never failed to take advantage of any man's folly. As for fame, Bacon hoped for it, even after death. 'Death hath this also', he said, 'that it openeth the gate to good fame and extinguisheth envy.' Surely nothing can sum him up better than this!

John Evelyn

1620–1706

THERE is a wonderfully calm, restful and dignified air about John Evelyn, and we always remember, as we read his diary, that he also wrote a treatise on forest trees. Indeed, that is how we think of him, walking through some leafy grove or plantation, or amongst the fountains and statues of some stately garden. He was acquainted with Kings and Queens, Ambassadors and noblemen, but he was no courtier; he liked best the life of a country squire. To plant trees, to design a garden, to plan the building or alteration of a country house; these were his interests, and even great men sought his advice on such matters. He was, in fact, as Pepys said 'a most excellent person . . . and must be allowed a little for a little conceitedness . . . But he may well be so, being a man so much above others.'

We, however, do not care a scrap whether Evelyn was conceited or not; we are more than grateful for his diary, and to find at least one man in those difficult times who kept his head and did not rant and roar, or go mad for an idea. He lived at a time when men were torn apart by conflicting passions; heads fell and loyalties were transferred with heat and bloodshed, but Evelyn remained calm and sane through all.

He was a Royalist at heart, yet he had personal friends in the Court of Cromwell and was on good terms with all. And why not? He consistently refused to take the Covenant, but that was no reason for quarrelling with old friends who did not share his views.

John Evelyn was born at Wotton, Surrey, on 31st October, 1620, the son of a rich country squire whose fortunes were connected with the manufacture of gunpowder. In the family mansion, set in its own splendid park and gardens, Evelyn's father kept '116 servants in liveries, every one in green satin doublets' and 'divers gentlemen and persons of quality in attendance in the same garb and habit'.

But the boy was simply brought up, and received his first lessons from the village schoolmaster. Later he went to Balliol College, Oxford, being at this time (he says) 'of a raw, vaine, uncertain and very unwary inclination'. But he soon came to real grips with life, for within four years he was an orphan, and the country had plunged into that long struggle between King Charles and his people which was to become civil war. On a bright May day Evelyn was present at the execution of the Earl of Strafford on Tower Hill, and a few weeks later Evelyn decided, like so many others, to go abroad.

It was at about this time that he began to keep a diary, chiefly, we gather, because his father had done the same. But this diary, unlike so many others, was not a book of confessions; he did not attempt to unburden his soul; it was a record of events, and set down with reserve, restraint and an admirable serenity, We, who now share it, find ourselves, therefore, taking on the same cool composure. We are rarely moved to laughter, we sometimes even wish to shake him out of his complacency, yet we return to this book because it is as soothing as the green shade of an English garden; it is a sanctuary from the rush of everyday life.

Our first journey with Evelyn is through Holland, but soon we make our bow to the Queen of Bohemia and the Court of Brussels, we visit 'divers of the fairest palaces', saunter through Italy, inspect churches, and gaze with rapture at pictures and statues and gardens. The party consists of a few light-hearted young men and the poet Waller; there are many adventures: they play on the lute, practise their High Dutch and Spanish, and ride through beautiful woods. Sometimes they lie in damask beds and are treated like Emperors, and sometimes in a wretched inn where the beds are lousy. But it is the gardens and palaces which are so engrossing; Evelyn in particular cannot tear himself away.

JOHN EVELYN
and his signature

It was thus that his excellent taste was formed. There were accidents, of course. He caught small-pox from an infected bed, and his valet robbed him of clothes and plate worth £60. But in Paris he met the young girl who was to become his wife. She was the daughter of the English Ambassador to France, Sir Richard Browne, and fifteen years old. They were married in 1647 on the Feast of Corpus Christi, so the streets were sumptuously hung with tapestry and strewn with flowers. A beautiful and memorable sight!

They lived together, first in Paris, and later in England, but in order to fit his young bride for the duties of a married woman Evelyn sent her a long treatise (thirteen chapters) on the ethics of marriage, including an essay, from a French writer, on the nuptial bed. The manuscript was beautifully bound in red leather and bore Evelyn's arms and motto. He warned his wife to keep it under lock and key and to show it to no one.

And now begins the real interest of the diary—the picture of social life during the Commonwealth and Restoration. For finally, of course, Evelyn came back to England, although the country was entirely in the hands of the rebels. He was tired of his exile and had decided to 'compound with the soldiers' and settle down at Sayes Court, a gabled Elizabethan manor-house at Deptford which belonged to his father-in-law. He sent for his young bride from France, and at Rye, one summer's afternoon, as he was playing at bowls, he watched her ship come sailing into harbour. She had by good fortune escaped the Dutch fleet and brought with her 'seventeen bailes of furniture'.

And so began that admirable family life of which he gives such an excellent account in his diary. Children were born (he had nine children) and were christened by the famous Dr Jeremy Taylor; sisters were married (and died in childbed), brothers were paired off, gardens were planted, houses were altered and improved. Sometimes, of course, some strange occurrence broke the monotony. A whale, fifty-six feet long came up the Thames; then there was a fearful tempest, and trees and chimneys came crashing down in all directions. The severe winters, too, apparently exceeded everything on record; the crows' feet were frozen to their prey and 'islands of ice enclosed both fish and fowl frozen, and some persons in their boats'. As for Evelyn, he was never idle. He seldom retired before midnight and rarely closed his eyes before one a.m. He was continually being asked to advise on architecture, the design of a garden or the care of woodlands or bees. He wrote books on History, Jesuitism and even a play, he dined and supped frequently with Lords, Ambassadors and Bishops; for soon, of course, Cromwell (that 'arch-rebel') was dead; there was no longer, as Evelyn said, 'anarchy and confusion'. One did not have to fall on one's knees night after night and pray 'Lord have mercy upon us'.

With the Restoration, indeed, it was possible to resume all the delightful diversions of the pre-Cromwellian era. Soon, therefore, Evelyn bought a coach, and in summer, with a family party, they would tour the country and visit cathedrals, churches, castles, ancient monasteries and 'gentlemen's faire houses'. He knew many of the owners of these country seats personally, and was shown everything—the picture gallery, the treasures collected abroad, the fine plate, the exquisite ivories and porcelain. The owner would beg him to taste of the wine from the vineyard, and offer him 'a handsome collation'. But when the inevitable 'avenue of trees' was 'ungraceful', and the seat 'naked', it distressed Evelyn; he could so easily have put matters right.

Occasionally he and his friends would make a round tour of seven hundred miles, but generally Mrs Evelyn remained at home, for she was continually expecting another child. And then, sometimes, there was a tragedy. 'A most likely child' would be 'overlayne' by the nurse.

One of Evelyn's sons, in particular, comes vividly before us, a boy who was a 'prodigy, and for beauty of body a very angel'. He could read before he was five, decline all the nouns, conjugate the verbs regular, turn English into Latin, construe and prove what he read and 'had a strong passion for Greek'. He had a wonderful disposition for mathematics, and could demonstrate propositions of Euclid. He was 'all life and all prettinesse', but he became very ill. 'Sweete Jesus, save me, deliver me, pardon my sins, let thine angels receive me', he cried, in the agony of his pain.

When he died Evelyn thought that he was 'suffocated by the women and maids that tended him, and covered him too hot with blankets as he lay in a cradle, near an excessive hot fire in a close roome'. It is indeed impossible to think of this child without utter sadness, for no boy could have been such a prodigy without excessive teaching, at the expense, of course, of the freedom and happy outdoor life so essential to a child. Such, apparently, was the ignorance of the times.

But our glimpse of Evelyn's household is only an occasional one; there are no records (as with Pepys) of quarrels, or the dismissal or misdeeds of servants; there are none of the petty annoyances that can disturb domestic life. We can only surmise, in fact, that his servants, in their green satin doublets, behaved with perfect decorum. As for food (which figures so largely in many diaries) it would seem that Evelyn barely noticed what he ate; it is never mentioned.

But Evelyn had far more important matters on hand, as he attended Councils of State, sat on many royal Commissions, and finally became Commissioner for the Sick and Wounded in the Dutch war, in which capacity he had to travel in all weathers, by land and water. It was a depressing and unrewarding task, as his own expenses were rarely repaid, and the Government begrudged every penny for the sick seamen. Magistrates and Justices, too, terrified of infection, persistently refused to admit the sick men anywhere, and sometimes they lay in the streets, begging for pity and imploring someone to knock them on the head. Often they 'died like dogs in the street unregarded'. In vain did Evelyn urged the Government to build an Infirmary for them at Chatham; but money again was apparently the obstacle.

And this, of course, is what we admire so much about Evelyn —his equanimity and patience. When things went wrong he did not meet them with bitterness and invective. We remember, for instance, that one hot summer's day, as he was riding in the country alone, he was set on by two rogues, who unhorsed him' took his money, sword and jewellery, bound him hand and foot, threw him into a thicket and threatened to cut his throat if he cried out. It was a lonely spot, and he was 'greviously tormented by flies', ants and the hot sun, but after struggling for two hours he managed to get free. When one of these robbers was caught and tried, Evelyn refused to give evidence against him, knowing that he would probably be hanged.

We cannot fail to admire Evelyn, too, for his work in the Great Fire. He helped, at some risk, to quench it, but when it was over 'God grant mine eyes may never behold the like', he said. Later on, Evelyn walked through the streets for hours, clambering over ruins and the heaps of burning rubbish; and thirteen days later he presented the King with a survey and 'a plot for a new citty', a remarkable achievement in so short a time.

It was pleasant, of course, to be of service to the King, yet there was behaviour at Court which shocked and horrified Evelyn. He could not but deplore the 'luxurious dallying and prophaneness' and the 'gaming and dissoluteness'. He knew the King well, as they had been exiles together. Evelyn had sailed with him in his yacht, breakfasted with him, and on one occasion held the candle as the King sat for his portrait. The King frequently consulted him when he was re-building his palace or altering his gardens. Evelyn had also introduced to His Majesty that extraordinary genius, Grinling Gibbons, whom he had discovered one winter's day in a poor thatched cottage carving a large crucifix. Evelyn had been so struck by the marvellous workmanship that he had knocked at the door and introduced himself. Later on the young carver was introduced to Sir Christopher Wren, and his exquisite work had been used in St Paul's Cathedral and many palaces, churches and great houses.

It was in middle age that Evelyn became very attached to Margaret Blagge, one of the Maids of Honour at Court. She was young enough to be his daughter, and from all accounts both beautiful and good. She used to consult him in her spiritual difficulties, as apparently at one time she had wished to become a nun. He drew up for her a scheme of devotion, and they used frequently to pray together by candle-light. He also wrote meditations for her, and she, poor child, used to pin up a slip of paper in her own room to remind her of special duties and prayers.

It was a strange friendship, and there can be little doubt that Evelyn was deeply in love with this charming girl, but her very innocence apparently protected her. She appears from their correspondence to have been utterly unworldly, and even the thought of marriage seemed a betrayal of her faith and duty to God. Finally, after many heart-searchings, and rather against Evelyn's advice, she married Sidney Godolphin, but all three remained friends, and Evelyn continued to dine with her almost every week.

Margaret Godolphin died shortly after giving birth to her first child, and to Evelyn it was a great tragedy. Of what use was it now to go to Court? He was not popular there, for the Maids of Honour said that he had 'a forbidding countenance' and reminded them too much of a schoolmaster. It was true, of course. He was very learned and serious, and he took it for granted—as such men do—that others were equally knowledgeable. When, for instance, the Marquess of Argyle mistook the turtle-doves in Evelyn's aviary for owls, Evelyn was so amazed and pained that he made a special note of it in his diary.

Considering the times, Evelyn lived to a great age (eighty-five), and he continued to keep his diary until a few weeks before his death. He retained, too, his quiet sense of humour, for one Sunday morning, when it was too wet to go to church, he asked his chaplain to take the service. The learned divine spoke in his sermon of the vanity of this world and the uncertainty of life, 'with pertinent inferences to prepare us for death and a future state'. 'I gave him thanks', said Evelyn, 'and told him I tooke it kindly as my funeral sermon.'

One of the last entries in Evelyn's diary is 'Divers of our friends and relations dined with us this day.' It was New Year's Eve, and they were, of course, 'very merry'. So that is our last glimpse of him, sitting at his hospitable table, a kindly, venerable old man who has lived a long time and had many sorrows, but still likes to give a family party. He died at Wotton, where he was born, in that splendid house with the Jacobean chimneys and stone-mullioned windows. Time has laid a soft mellowing hand on the fine red brickwork, on the bell towers and romantic moat and bridge; the great oak gates have weathered almost to ribbons, but the well-wrought iron bolts and hinges stand fast. The great hall, too, finely decorated with plaster carvings and coats of arms, is as handsome as ever. But it is the lovely romantic garden which reminds us most of Evelyn, for here is something dream-like; the magnolia trees open their pure flowers to the air, the great dark yews and stately cypresses stand watch over the emerald lawns; there are statues, a fountain, a grotto, exquisite blossoming trees. There is a massive stone temple, decaying, but very lovely in conception. Here, indeed, is an atmosphere of pure magic, and it was created chiefly by Evelyn himself. We walk down the narrow lane leading to the tiny church which Evelyn and his family must have used hundreds of times; and there, in a small chapel, are the memorials to Evelyn's mother and father, placed there by loving hands; there are five kneeling children, so solemn, so devout; it is a significant symbol of a bygone age.

George Fox

1624–1691

MACAULAY has said that George Fox the Quaker was far too crazy to be at large, yet we who can contemplate his extraordinary life from the serenity of our own age of religious toleration, are not so sure. It is true that he once walked up and down the streets of Lichfield shouting, 'Woe to the bloody city of Lichfield! Woe to the bloody city of Lichfield!' Yet he was not the only man in that curious age who got excited about religion; he merely had more courage than most of his contemporaries.

The wonderful example of heroism set by George Fox, in fact, is not only humbling but inspiring. For how many of us to-day would be prepared to stand firm in a hostile world, and to suffer incredible hardships for a burning faith?

Faith, of course, in the seventeenth century was a matter of life and death, for if one had the wrong faith one ran the risk of going to hell, but if one had the right faith the reward was heaven; so it was believed. To see one's fellow-creatures, therefore, heading for perdition and eternal damnation was not only an anxiety to the serious minded; it was a calamity.

To George Fox, a poor, uneducated shepherd, religion meant more than life itself. And he believed that his religion was the only true one. But to his profound distress the majority of people could not see it. They laughed and danced through life, and snapped their fingers at him. He was obliged, therefore, to point out to them the vanity and wickedness of their ways, but to his astonishment they reviled him. He was continually in a minority of one, misjudged, misunderstood and terribly alone. Why had he ever been born into such a blind and foolish world?

It is impossible to say how George Fox came to hold his strange opinions, but it must be remembered that he reached manhood at a time when rural England was in a state of religious ferment. Some of the religious movements which had started on the continent through the mighty vortex currents of the Reformation, had gradually and quietly invaded England, occasionally through the migration of a persecuted leader or group, and sometimes by the return home of chance visitors who had been 'infected' abroad.

But however the seed was sown, there can be no doubt that it fell on the most fertile ground, for even as a boy George Fox was not like other children. He was always 'most grave, serious and pious', and as a young man he became convinced that the Protestant religion was completely artificial. He believed that God was a living spiritual presence revealed within the soul, and he declared that he himself had come into direct contact with God. At the age of twenty-eight he had climbed 'a very high mountain', and there he had had a vision of the great work which had been chosen for him.

But to carry out this holy task he knew that he must speak out strongly. He therefore went constantly to the Law Courts to 'cry for justice', he wrote to judges and magistrates, he warned publicans against allowing people to drink too much, he protested vehemently against wakes, feasts, May-games, shows, weddings, wrestling, football, etc. He protested against cheating, cozening and lying, and he implored teachers to keep children from 'lightness, vanity and wantonness'.

But what saddened him most was to hear a church bell ring; it 'struck at his life'. He believed that every 'steeple-house' was an idol, so in the middle of the service he would enter a church and loudly abuse the parson. He would tell him that he was 'a painted beast in a painted house'. The result was pandemonium, and the people would 'fall upon Fox in a great rage'; they would beat him out of the church with sticks and bibles, etc. He would be put in the stocks, where he would be stoned and mocked. Time and again he was thrown out of the town and beaten, his

GEORGE FOX

clothes were torn off, rotten eggs were thrown at him, he was immersed in ponds and ditches, and kicked and trampled upon until he was barely able to stand. Drums and kettles were beaten to drown his voice, and sometimes he was put into 'a nasty stinking prison'.

Yet if these blind people believed that they could quench his spirit and move him from his purpose they were much mistaken, for as soon as he was released he continued in the same manner. He held meetings continually—preferably on top of a hill, where he felt nearer to God—and there, with tremendous earnestness and sometimes tears, he thundered forth his doctrine. His only wish was to turn people from darkness to light. But what terribly uphill work it was! When he told people that their hearts were rotten and that they were full of hypocrisy they were offended; he could not understand it. To one woman he said 'Thou hast been a harlot', and he told another that she was a witch (for he 'discerned an unclean spirit in her'). But she, too, was offended and left the room. It was a harrowing life. Yet he bore it meekly and with patience because he was certain that he was suffering in a good cause.

How difficult it had been for him, as a young man groping for the light! That period had been one of torment and anguish, for although as a shepherd he had been fairly happy—he had loved the solitude—yet when later he had been apprenticed to a shoe-maker 'boys and rude people' had ridiculed him mercilessly. At the age of nineteen, therefore, he had left home and started to tramp the country, hoping to find a priest who would understand his difficulties. But what a bitter quest this was! For having unburdened his heart to a likely priest he was advised merely to take tobacco and sing psalms—a piece of advice which enraged him, for 'Tobacco was a thing I did not love, and psalms I was not in a state to sing; I could not sing.' This unkind priest also repeated to his servants and the milkmaids all that George had said; it was too humiliating.

The world at that time had seemed, in fact, 'a briery, thorny wilderness,' and then at times 'like the great raging waves of the sea'. Oh, misery, misery! He walked 'abroad in solitary places many days', he fasted continually and sat in hollow trees. But it seemed to him that 'all was dark and under the chain of darkness,' so when it was day he wished for night and when it was night he wished for day. His 'temptations', too, were terrible, and sometimes he was 'tempted almost to despair'.

There were, however, other priests whom he was advised to consult, so George walked many miles to speak with a man of whom he had heard. Alas, as they were walking together in the priest's garden George happened to step on the side of a flower-bed, whereupon the priest raged at him 'as if his house had been on fire'. George went away in great sorrow, and decided that the priest was 'like an empty hollow cask'.

With priests he was particularly unfortunate, for another of that kin decided that George should be bled and given 'physick'. Yet they could not get one drop of blood from the poor wretched man, his body being (as he said) 'dried up with sorrow, griefs and troubles'. Indeed, he wished that he had never been born, or that he had been born deaf or blind, so that he might not know the vanity and wickedness that surrounded him.

It is clear, however, that George Fox gradually found comfort, for his influence, as he became more eloquent, cannot be doubted, and he made many converts. When he and his friends had had 'a glorious meeting', with many prayers and tears, he was filled with happiness. A wonderful peace would descend upon him; it was soft as dew, as calm as a summer's day. The 'truth had shined over all'. And he would go home to his frugal supper greatly comforted.

He and his followers called themselves The Society of Friends, and their religion was marked by an utter simplicity, without ritual, music, programme, sacraments or paraphernalia of any kind. They met in a plain building—when it was possible—and sat down together in silence, in complete confidence that the spirit would be a real presence amongst them. They were all kindly, civil, temperate people, ready always to turn the other cheek. They drank and ate abstemiously, they were neither touchy nor critical, and it was their creed that God did not dwell in temples built by men but in men's hearts. It was a creed which had much to recommend it to a certain type of mind.

George Fox never stayed in one town for any length of time in case he should be hurt or changed by talking to one person too much, but he soon became known, and as he rode towards the gates of a city on his horse people would point to him and whisper, 'The man in the leathern breeches is come.' Then, 'so dreadful was the power of God upon him' that they 'flew like chaff' before him into their shops and houses. Who can blame them? Some of his home-truths hit the mark fairly and squarely and were only too justified. Sometimes, too, when he felt moved to go into a church and interrupt the service, people were seen to tremble with fear, and 'some of them feared it would fall down on their heads'. There can be no doubt that he frequently caused a great uproar.

Many magistrates had a certain sympathy with the Quakers, for it was obvious that these people were passionately sincere; they merely wished to save those who were heading for perdition. But the law was the law, and it was the duty of magistrates and judges to administer it. George Fox believed that the Lord had forbidden him to take off his hat to anyone, of any class. When he was charged in Court, therefore, with holding unlawful meetings and disturbing the peace he refused to take off his hat. Nothing would induce him to do so, and the gaoler would thereupon remove the offending article. George Fox would calmly replace it. There was, in fact, such a taking-off and putting-on of hats that the judge must often have wondered why Quakers did not go bareheaded. Would not one problem then have been solved?

However, the Quakers were warned that if they persisted in breaking the laws they would be sent to prison; and so it was. The heavy gates would close upon them, the gaolers would put on the fetters, and there they would remain, sometimes for a year without being tried. At one time there were a thousand Quakers in prison simply for refusing to take the oath of allegiance, refusing to pay tithes, and to take off their hats. The prisons were sometimes so deep in mire that it was impossible to lie down, and on one occasion Fox was put into a damp, dripping tower, where the rain and the wind beat in, night and day. His limbs swelled, and he became very ill. In the prison at Carlisle he suffered horribly, for the gaolers were in 'a black dark rage' and continually beat him and his friends with great cudgels. They were determined to break his spirit, but they did not know George Fox, who merely commenced to sing. The enraged gaoler then brought in a fiddler to drown the noise of the singing, but Fox sang even louder.

Priests, too, endeavoured to make the Quaker see the error of his ways, and they came to prison to talk to him. Yet when they discovered that they could make no impression on this strange and obstinate man they became 'rude and devilish'. They too, believed that their religion was the only true one. No, he had nothing in common with the orthodox priests; these 'jangling professors' belonged to another world. Great ladies and countesses also came to visit him, and he was flattered and gratified, but never for one moment was he deflected from his purpose. He would save the world or die. So the moment he was released from prison he pulled on his boots and mounted his horse again. He rode from one town to another, in rain or snow, hail or shine, week after week, month after month, so that his message would ring right through the land. He made hundreds of converts, and wherever he created a little group of friends he knew that the seed would flourish and grow and spread. After a time, therefore, he could always find friends in any town; they received him with joy, and it was never difficult to arrange a meeting, although secrecy generally had to be observed. Fortunately a great part of the service was conducted in silence, but when Fox decided that they must pray, a small boy would be placed at the door to sing loudly and drown the voices. These wonderful meetings lifted him up into a state of utter sublimation, and more than compensated for all that he had suffered, or might have to suffer in the future.

As time passed George Fox mellowed considerably. Was it because he realised that his work was seriously hampered while he was in prison, or because he had discovered that quieter methods were more effective? It is hard to say. But at least he had not budged one inch from his rigid principles. He still insisted that it was wrong to say 'Goodmorrow' or 'Good evening', because that implied that God had made good days and bad days. He still refused to bow or 'scrape' to anyone; and 'junketing and feasting, chambering and wantonness' still grieved him deeply. As for ribbons, laces and 'costly apparel', one could only avert one's eyes and pray that those who wore such frivolities would not find hell too painful.

'Repent! Repent!' was his cry, and his big, resonant voice could be heard in markets, fairs, squares and public assemblies. 'For your soul's sake repent!' Some simple peasants, in fact, began to believe that he was a prophet, with the power to heal, so they brought to him their crippled children and their mad relatives. He did what he could for each one, and sometimes he was convinced that he had the power of healing.

In the meantime, he was anxious to meet the great Cromwell and to plead for his friends, many of whom were still languishing in dungeons. One morning, therefore, he was brought before the Protector at the palace of Whitehall, and they had a long talk, not apparently without result, for as Fox was leaving the room Cromwell caught him by the hand and with tears in his eyes said, 'Come again to my house, for if thou and I were but an hour of a day together we should be nearer one to the other.' On another occasion the Quaker met Cromwell in the park and warned him solemnly that 'they that would put a crown on him would take away his life'. Should he not 'mind the crown that was immortal'? Later on Fox met the Protector in Hampton Court Park as he rode at the head of his lifeguard, and again he reminded him of the sufferings of the Quakers in prison. Could not something be done for them? Was it justice that they should be so cruelly treated? 'But', said Fox, 'I saw and felt a waft of death go forth against him, and when I came to him he looked like a dead man.' So much for Cromwell, the great Protector. George had wished to describe his own misery and privations in prison; he had wanted to tell him that through his sufferings he had lost both hearing and sight for several weeks. Ah, there was so much he could have said . . . But there was no time; the great man was surrounded by his soldiers; he was holding England by the power of the sword. What should he know or care of a poor Quaker? Besides, even in prison there were compensations. His very sufferings sometimes brought wonderful visions; and always, both night and day, he was supported by the knowledge that he had staunch unwavering friends in every town in England. Had not others before him been burnt alive at the stake for their faiths? They had perished joyfully. If necessary he was prepared to do the same.

So time passed, and the passage of the years brought to Fox the realisation that the seed was 'pretty well sown in England'. Could he not go further afield and spread his glorious doctrine in other lands? In Ireland, for instance, he had heard that there was appalling ignorance and depravity and darkness. Oh, to bring the heavenly light to those poor deluded souls. Surely all the bells in heaven would ring if he could persuade them to see what was so plain, so clear! To Ireland, therefore, he sailed, but as soon as he went ashore at Dublin he smelt (as he said) 'the corruption of the nation, so that it gave another smell to me than England did'. No, he did not like Ireland, and he did not stay long.

Yet would there not be a chance in Scotland? The Scots were a godfearing, simple people to whom surely his message would appeal. Indeed, when first he arrived in Scotland he 'felt the seed of God to sparkle about him like innumerable sparks of fire'. Was not this a good sign and an excellent beginning? Lady Margaret Hamilton and a certain Earl were particularly interested. His visit, however, was not a successful one, and eventually he was ordered to leave the country.

As for marriage, what had such a partnership to do with a man who had no permanent home, and whose sole aim in life was the saving of souls? Nevertheless, there was a lady who had been converted to Quakerism and whom he grew to love. She was the widow of Judge Fell, and in the year 1669 she and

George Fox were married. They lived for only a week together and then parted, each to continue their serious work. He wrote to her as 'My dear Heart in the Truth and Life that changeth not', and they were often parted, for she too went to prison many times.

It was two years after his marriage that Fox set sail for America, in a boat which proved to be so rotten and leaky that the passengers and seamen were obliged to pump night and day, all through the voyage. They were at sea for seven weeks and some odd days, finally landing at Barbados, where George Fox, with his usual courage, gave the natives much advice, in no uncertain terms. He particularly warned them against being cruel to their slaves, and advised them to set them free after a number of years.

After Barbados he and his friends went to Jamaica, and then to Maryland, from whence they travelled right through America, over woods, wildernesses and bogs. They swam their horses over great foaming rivers, travelled miles by canoe, camped in the forests and slept in Indians' wigwams. They escaped the perils of wolves, bears, tigers, lions, rattlesnakes and man-eaters. But his visit was highly successful and he made many converts. He warned the Indians solemnly that if they did evil they would be burnt—presumably in hell—and he never spared those of whom he disapproved.

Later, on his return to England, he paid a visit to Holland with William Penn, and also went into Germany, where he wrote warnings to the people of several towns.

George Fox died on 13th January, 1691, bravely and cheerfully, and it is said that four thousand Friends were present at his burial. He had spent many years in prison and his health had suffered severely as a result of his many hardships, and long and fatiguing journeys. Nevertheless he had continued to organise the affairs and meetings of the Society of Friends all over the world almost to the time of his death. There can be no doubt that he was deeply lamented, and his example of courage and endurance was a magnificent inspiration.

As an individual whose influence was so profound and far-reaching there are few to equal him. His fanaticism may seem deplorable, but in his age it was necessary to raise one's voice in order to be heard at all, for the artisan ånd the peasant did not count; they had no votes and no influence. They were regarded as less than the dust, and only the rich and noble had any power. George Fox showed what could be achieved even by a humble shepherd. It must be remembered, too, that he had no axe to grind. For himself he asked nothing—neither fame, riches or power, and if ever a man deserved to wear an immortal crown it was he.

John Bunyan

1628–1688

'AS I walked through the wilderness of this world I lighted upon a certain place where there was a den, and I laid me down in that place to sleep; and as I slept I dreamed a dream.'

Thus are we introduced to that wonderful allegory, *The Pilgrim's Progress*, a book which has placed John Bunyan, the Bedfordshire tinker, amongst the Immortals. And what a remarkable opening is here, for this simple statement arrests our interest at once, and before we know what has happened we are deeply immersed in this beautiful allegory, this pilgrimage of the soul. We are led by the hand through valleys and over mountains, through meadows of lilies, past sheepfolds and flowering orchards, through swamps and snares and pitfalls. There is the burning pit with its hideous shapes, the horrible castle with its courtyard paved with the skulls of pilgrims; there is the wicket gate and the desolate swamp, the palace, the cross and the sepulchre, the steep hill and the pleasant arbour; there is the green valley of humiliation, the little hill by the silver mine and the pleasant river. And finally there is the land of Beulah with its flowers and singing birds, where the sun shines night and day. Then on the other side of that black and cold river over which there is no bridge, we see the golden pavements and streets of pearl.

But this vision is not only a pilgrimage; it is shot through and through with human interest. For was any man in fiction ever so real as Christian, staggering and toiling under his awful burden? How we groan with him in his struggles! How we long to ease him of his heavy load! We can feel the oppressive weight of it ourselves bearing us down as we struggle in the bog and the river. We despair with him, we rejoice with him.

But perhaps the most remarkable thing about this great book is that it was written in prison; every character and scene came hot from the brain of this tinker. He had no fine library stuffed with classics to inspire him, and no pleasant travels in distant lands to look back on. England was the only country he knew, and of books he possessed only two—*The Bible* and *The Book of Martyrs*. He and his fellow prisoners slept on straw in miserably cold cells; he read and wrote by the light of a candle or a cheap rushlight, and there was neither chair nor stool. Yet he was obliged to pay a weekly sum for lodgings and sheets, also turn-keys' fees, a heavy sum for the privilege of not wearing irons, and 'garnish money'. This was his environment; this is where his dream was conceived and set down. And he was in prison solely because he refused to stop preaching. The prison in Bedford in which Bunyan wrote *The Pilgrim's Progress* was built on one of those ancient 'fayre stone bridges' which were such a feature of England in the seventeenth century. Five arches spanned the river Ouse, and the prison was also a toll-house. The river, therefore, gurgling and murmuring between the arches, could be seen from Bunyan's cell; he could see, also, a small island covered with shrubs and greenery. In spring it blossomed in beauty; in winter its dead vegetation floated desolately in the water, and the brown reeds rustled mournfully in the wind. These sounds and sights were his daily companions, yet it is safe to say that they barely encroached on his consciousness, for he wrote continually. During his twelve years in gaol he produced many books, all concerned with religion, all showing a way of life. The words came pouring forth, and it was imperative that they should be set down, for he was forbidden to preach; that is why he was in prison. He had a wife and a family of young children, one of whom was blind. They were terribly poor, and often in desperate plight, but he had made his choice; rather than submit to the law and refuse to preach he stayed behind bars.

JOHN BUNYAN
From the painting by Thomas Sadler, 1684

He was utterly convinced that what he was doing was right. This was John Bunyan, and that he was in deadly earnest cannot be doubted.

John Bunyan was, in fact, one of the saddest victims of the religious persecution of the seventeenth century, a persecution which to-day seems as senseless as it was cruel. But the religion of England at that time was decided by the Government, and it had been laid down that England was to be a Protestant country. All who refused to accept this rigid creed, therefore, were regarded as 'heretics', 'traitors', 'mockers', 'scoffers', etc. They could be men and women of the highest morals and of the most blameless life, but whether they were Puritans, Catholics, Quakers or other sects they were all equally vulnerable. This very persecution, however, roused in men a determination to stand firm by their principles and to suffer gladly the most fearful hardships. It was the price one paid for one's beliefs, and as the martyrs of old had died happily at the stake while the flames hissed round them, so were the dissenters determined, if necessary, to do likewise. A man like Bunyan, who was burning with religious ardour, could not keep silent, but by the authorities it was believed that he was deliberately drawing men from the true faith, and so jeopardising the salvation of their souls. This was the law of the land, and must be obeyed.

Spies, in fact, were employed all over the country ruthlessly to hunt down the peaceable people who attended these dissenters' meetings. The spies were paid sometimes as much as £15 for a single successful conviction, and they would watch at night, climb trees and range the woods for hours. The dissenters, therefore, held their meetings where they could—in barns, in the middle of a wood, or in the roof of an old house. Here the pious worshippers, disguised, and under cover of darkness, would gather together to pray, to talk, and to hear some eloquent preacher. If they were discovered they were arrested and heavily fined; their goods, furniture, and even the very tools with which they earned their living were taken away. Corn would be cut and carted away, horses would be driven off, and cattle seized. Yet as a rule the offenders were poor peasants—carpenters, tinkers, farmers, blacksmiths.

Let us look at John Bunyan, however, before he had been sent to prison, before he had achieved that remarkable faith. As a boy he had been anything but religious, and was much addicted to cursing, swearing and blaspheming. He was fond of bell-ringing, field sports and dancing, recreations which he came to regard as 'grievous sins' when he became a Puritan. His 'conversion', however, took some years, but when first he realised with horror that he was living a 'sinful' life he went through a long period of utter misery and despair. 'Oh, no one knows the terrors of those days but myself', he confessed later. There was no peace for him, night or day. 'My soul was driven as with the winds', he said. 'I was as those that jostle against the rocks.' His agony of spirit, in fact, cannot be measured, for he shook and trembled, and sometimes he felt too ill even to weep. 'I would have given a thousand pounds for a tear' he said. Sometimes he felt that his breastbone was splitting in two, and this he believed to be a sign that he was destined to 'burst asunder like Judas'. His sleep, too, was haunted by fearful dreams, in which he saw horrible devils, evil spirits and hell-fire. Indeed, often he wished that he himself was a devil so that he might be a tormenter and not tormented.

Bunyan married at the age of twenty, and he and his young wife were so poor that they 'had not a dish or a spoon between them'. But his wife brought with her two precious books (left to her by her father)—*The Plain man's pathway to Heaven* and *The Practice of Piety*, both of which were new to Bunyan. He pored over the Bible, too, night and day, and the more he read the more he was convinced of his own wickedness; in his own eyes he was 'more loathsome than a toad'; he felt that he had committed the unpardonable sin against the Holy Ghost and so was utterly damned and lost. 'My soul is dying! My soul is damning!' he groaned. 'What shall I do to be saved?' What shall I do? What shall I do? The phrase echoed through his brain like a hammer night and day, and he felt that 'the very sun in the heaven did grudge to give (him) light' and 'the very stones in the streets . . . banded themselves against (him)'. 'Methought that they all combined to banish me out of the world. I was abhorred of them and unfit to dwell among them because I had sinned against the Saviour', he said.

His misery, in fact, for nearly three years was terrible, and in his search for comfort he turned frantically again and again to the Bible. But there was little comfort there: 'Simon, Simon, behold Satan hath desired to have you', he read. And then, 'The wicked are like the troubled sea, when it cannot rest, whose waters cast up mire and dirt. There is no peace, saith God, to the wicked.' Merciful heavens, this was unbearable! And then he read: 'But he that shall blaspheme against the Holy Ghost hath never forgiveness, but is in danger of eternal damnation.'

Was not this proof positive that he was damned? Damned for ever. Was not this the reason for his strange and terrifying visions? Possibly he was already possessed of a devil, for had he not frequently felt him pulling at his clothes behind him, and although he would savagely spurn with his foot and strike with his hands against the 'destroyer', that evil thing would return again and again. Sometimes, indeed, he felt that it would be best to sell himself to the devil; then the matter would be at an end. . . . Yet there were straws to snatch at, for did not the Bible also say, 'Thou art my love, thou art my dove'? How beautiful that was! And did it not indicate a shred of hope for him? 'Thou art my love, thou art my dove', said the Bible. 'But is it true, is it true?' whispered the devil at his elbow.

And so through the 'vale of darkness and desolation' Bunyan came at length to his fruitful land of Beulah. Tossed and buffeted, worn and exhausted, he found some measure of peace at last. And then, of course, he was determined that others should also be saved. They too must be rescued from those pits of darkness, those tormenting devils. And there was no time to be lost. Did not the young girls and youths still play and dance round the market cross on the village green, wasting their foolish time in

May games and other frivolities? They spent their holidays in utter wantonness, when they should have been praying, singing psalms and thinking of the next life. How it grieved him! How it pained him to see the flags and gay ribbons hanging from the maypole, and the young people swarming off to the fair, with all its vanities and foolishness, its bear-baiting, and cock-fighting, and wrestling, and clowns! Oh vanity, vanity, all was vanity!

Bunyan spent altogether twelve long years in gaol, and later another short period of six months. But during that time many efforts were made to secure his release, or to obtain for him a fair trial. His wife, Elizabeth, although miserably poor and burdened with a large family (she had married him when he was a widower with four young children) was tireless in her efforts to present petitions on his behalf. She even went to London— a serious journey for a peasant woman in those days—to deliver a petition to the judge personally. But nothing came of her pitiful plea. Later, at the Bedford Assizes, she presented two petitions to the judges. And finally, on the Sheriff's advice, the young Puritan, in her plain grey gown and snowy apron and cap, went to the Swan chamber, where the two judges and many justices and gentry of the county were sitting together. With a quaking heart she made her way through this fine company and courageously faced Sir Matthew Hale. 'My Lord, I make bold to come once again to your lordship', she said, and with all the grace and charm of a young woman she pleaded eloquently for her husband. She pointed out that he had not been lawfully convicted. Could he not, at least, be given a fair trial? Besides, she had young children, one of whom was blind, and her husband was prevented from earning for them what they needed. He was a man of genius and fine feeling; his preaching could hurt no one. He merely wished to show men a better way of life. 'My lord, my lord', she begged, with tears in her eyes, 'I beg you to inter-cede for me.'

But although she was received with kindness, nothing was done for Bunyan. He, in the meantime, did what he could to assist his family, and he made thousands of gross of tagged laces.

When the candle in his cell was guttering and the faint light of dawn came creeping in through his tiny barred window he was still at work. He was often in tears at the thought of his young wife and her heavy burden, but his duty to God came first; man-made laws were a mere trifle compared with one's sacred beliefs. Was not that immortal crown worth winning? Had it not been promised? God was watching every step. He knew; He knew.

There was one matter, however, which troubled Bunyan. He had little doubt that eventually he would be hanged; and of course he would not be the first. Many Catholics, only a few years ago, had been stretched on the rack, put to the treadmill and finally hanged or beheaded. Bunyan was not afraid to die, but he dreaded that when that solemn moment came he might climb the ladder with a pale face and tottering knees. That would be a sad disgrace; it would show that he could not bear up through the word of God; it would prove that he himself had no hope of immortality, that he was afraid to meet his Maker. . . . However, if he was hanged, he hoped at least that he would be able to give a message of life to those who came to see him die, for if he could convert but one soul through his last words his life would not be in vain.

It was as a result of the Declaration of Indulgence that Bunyan was at last released from gaol. This declaration suspended by royal prerogative the execution of all penal laws in matters ecclesiastical against all Nonconformists or Recusants. Bunyan, therefore, was a free man (although he was to spend a further short period in prison later) and his real work could now begin. He resumed his preaching, and became a 'teacher' or minister of religion attached to the 'Congregational' Church. He had borne his tedious imprisonment, often under cruel and oppressive gaolers, with exemplary patience, and his reward had come.

The Pilgrim's Progress, written in Bunyan's last short period of imprisonment, was an immediate success, and found its way not only into the libraries of the most fastidious scholars and critics, but into the most humble cottages. It was a book which even children and the illiterate could love and appreciate, for here was a universality of thought which recommended it to every man and woman. It was a tale told with the utmost simplicity, yet it contained some of the highest qualities of the great ancient masters, a completeness, a dramatic unity, and a rare force and beauty. There were no signs of labour, and the vision had opened out like a flower, fresh and effortless. We cannot doubt for a moment, in fact, that Bunyan was carried away by his own inspiration, that he lived to the full his own strange dream. He, too, had laughed, and trembled, and sighed, with poor Christian.

There were, of course, the usual foolish critics who declared that Bunyan the tinker could not have written this book. But surely they could never have heard the man preach! For it was not Bunyan's fame alone which, when he went to London to preach, brought a congregation of literally thousands of people; his eloquence was fanatically admired. Sometimes he could barely reach his pulpit for the crowds, and had to be carried over the heads of men.

It was inevitable, too, that as a public figure—for his many books had brought him great fame—he was criticised, and that envious tongues tried to belittle him. It was whispered that he was a witch, a Jesuit and a highwayman, and that he had his whores and bastards, statements so fantastic that Bunyan was merely amused. For surely such libels had always been the lot of famous men through the centuries!

In appearance Bunyan was tall, strong and ruddy, with sparkling eyes. He wore a moustache, 'after the old British fashion', his hair was reddish, his forehead high. He dressed very plainly, and although he looked like a man 'of stern and rough temper' his conversation was mild and affable, modest, quiet, and friendly. He wrote, altogether, sixty books, including that remarkable autobiography *Grace abounding to the chief of sinners*.

Samuel Pepys

1633–1703

IT is impossible to remember the Restoration, and picture
Charles II and his elegant court without seeing the figure of
Samuel Pepys, the diarist, handsomely dressed and bewigged,
looking smilingly upon the company. For he loved, more than
anything, to go to Whitehall and 'walk among the courtiers . . .
being now beginning to be pretty well known among them'.
He had the entrée, of course, for he was for many years Secretary
to the Navy Office; the King and the Duke of York often sought
his advice, and he sat in Council continually with many of the
great officers of State.

But this is merely one of the pictures of Pepys. We see him
perhaps even more clearly, presiding over one of his dinner-
parties in his handsome wainscoted dining-room. There would be
what he called 'an abundance of candles lit' and the table was
loaded with succulent food; the immaculate cloth was set with
gleaming silver plate and his two beautiful silver flagons. There
would be four fiddlers to play, and then the company would
'fall to cards'. Later on, if the night was warm and fine, he and his
guests would go out on to the leads and make music and sing.
Music enchanted him; he confessed that he was 'almost ravished'
by it, and he himself could play the triangle, the flageolet, the lute
and the flute.

Yet perhaps the first picture that comes to mind is of Pepys
in his early married life before he had made his way. We see him
in their little garret in Axe Yard, with his pretty young French
wife; she was the daughter of a French Huguenot who had been
gentleman carver to Queen Henrietta. Pepys and his wife were so

poor then that she used to do the washing and 'make coal fires, poor wretch'. Then suddenly all was changed, for Pepys sailed with Lord Sandwich to Holland to fetch King Charles II back to England, for the Restoration of the Monarchy. The company put on clothes 'as rich as silver and gold could make them', and then began to drink, and to eat oysters. They played ninepins, they sang lustily, the guns boomed all day, there were 'silk flags and scarlet waistcloaths', there were trumpeters and fiddlers playing their heads off. Meanwhile, the State arms on the ship were pulled down and the ship's painters set up the King's arms instead. And finally the King and all his suite came on board. A great moment, indeed!

It was the Restoration, in fact, which brought Pepys into the limelight. He who was the son of a poor tailor (although he had been educated at St Paul's School and Cambridge) was given a good post under Lord Sandwich, a post that he fulfilled extremely well. He worked early and late, and set a splendid example of efficiency. Yet there was time for many other interests, too. The theatre he loved (and could not understand how others did not share his taste); books he loved, also, and in time collected a fine library. But to dine with great men and take part in their 'noble discourse' delighted him most, for he had an excellent brain and his curiosity was insatiable.

There can be no question that Samuel Pepys was an admirable companion, as he was interested in everything; he was strong and fearless; he knew his own mind and he had no complexes; if he had a problem he soon solved it and quickly recovered his equanimity. He had the kindest heart, and was keenly alive to the beauty, the drama, the poetry and the humour of life. He was easily moved to tears and the sight of suffering made him tremble and weep. He loved children, too (alas, he had none of his own!). But above all, he was intensely human. For instance, he always did his shopping and drank his beer where there was a pretty woman, and he rarely failed to steal a kiss or two before leaving. As for parties, there can be no doubt that he entered wholeheartedly into all the fun. 'My Lady Pen flung me down upon the

SAMUEL PEPYS
From the painting by John Hayls

bed', he says, 'and herself and others one after another upon me, and very merry we were.' On another occasion there were fireworks, and the guests threw their rockets and squibs at each other, smutting each other with candle-grease and soot 'till most of us,' he confesses, 'were like devils'. There was nothing half-hearted about Pepys.

We must remember, of course, that at this time men and women had become utterly weary of the hard Commonwealth regime; now they were determined to enjoy life again. Pepys worked hard and played hard. He thought it necessary, also, in order to keep his position, to 'make a show'. Clothes, therefore, were extremely important. He chose his own fine suits and his wife's dresses with the greatest care, and he put his servants into splendid liveries. When at last he could afford to keep his own coach he was the proudest man in London. He drove round and round the ring in Hyde Park, bowing to his friends with as much dignity as if he had been born a Prince of the Blood Royal. Pepys also had a delicious sense of humour. 'But Lord', he says, on one occasion, 'the mirth which it caused me to be waked in the night by this snoring round about me; I did laugh till I was ready to burst.' No one else, we feel, would have laughed.

The confessions he makes, in fact, are so human that our sympathy goes right out to him; we live in his presence. And much as we deplore his infidelities and his amorous adventures, he is always so repentant that we cannot but forgive him; it was a licentious age. Besides, there is not a scrap of malice, or bitterness, or treachery about Pepys. It was his *joie de vivre* alone that was responsible for his faults.

His diary was not, of course, intended for others to read (it was all written in his own secret shorthand); he merely wished to keep a private record, not only of events, but of his own shortcomings, so that he might improve. That is why he continually made vows—against women, drink, theatre-going, etc. When they were 'out' he had his fling for a day or two, and then 'fell to them again', reading them over every Sunday night.

No, we cannot possibly dislike Pepys for his faults. His vanity, in fact, is merely amusing, and his jealousy concerning his wife is pathetic, for there is no doubt that he suffered; he could not sleep or work while it continued.

It is not, of course, for the revelation of character alone that we value this wonderful diary, but for the vivid picture he paints of the life of his day. We are shown, in addition to Court life, the outlook, manners and behaviour of the artisan class—Pepys's father (the tailor), his garrulous, ill-tempered mother, his sister Pall (a thorn in the flesh!), who stole his wife's scissors and his maid's book. Pepys was secretly ashamed of his poor relations after he had risen in the world, yet he often asked them to dinner. Their plebeian manners and foolish conversation pained and depressed him, but he bore with it. Sometimes he would take them to Spring Gardens, where one could hear 'the nightingale and other birds and fiddles and a harp, and a Jew's trump'. This was 'mighty divertising'. And here 'the wenches would gather pinks' and his pageboy would creep through a hedge to pick 'an abundance of roses'. They would eat cakes and powdered beef and drink ale, then by 'brave moonshine' go home by water. As for my Lady Sandwich, there is no doubt that she was fond of Pepys; sometimes when her Lord was away Samuel would go and sit with her in her chamber and talk; and when she called on him to see his house and garden he would lead her through the court by the hand, 'she being very fine and her page carrying up her train'.

Indeed, the picture Pepys paints for us is so complete that it is better than anything a novelist could do. He had eyes for everything—the children picking up rags in the street (for a living), the fine ladies walking in Gray's Inn Walk, the Duke of York 'talking wantonly' with his mistress (Mrs Palmer) through the curtains of Whitehall Chapel, Nell Gwynn standing smiling at the door of her lodging, lords and ladies at Court dancing a country dance, the monkeys climbing the ropes at St Batholomew's Fair. It is all as clear as if we ourselves were present; there are passages in the diary, too, of extreme beauty. His description of his meeting with a shepherd on Epsom Downs, for instance, is as brilliant as anything in English literature. And no one has described so vividly the Restoration, the Coronation of the King, the horrors of the plague and the fire of London. It was he who advised the King to order houses to be pulled down during the fire in order to prevent it spreading further. He behaved with much courage, too, during the plague, in deciding to stay in London and continue with his work; and it is through his eyes that we see the deserted city, the grass growing in Whitehall Court, the river empty of boats, and 'none but poor wretches in the streets'. The plague, he says, made people 'cruel as doggs one to another'. Yet even here he makes us smile, for he confesses that he decided to break his vows against drink because his doctor (whose advice he felt obliged to take) was dead of the plague, and his surgeon out of the way.

Thus is the picture built up, and the very pulse of life is in it. We see the Lord Chancellor and Judges riding on horseback to Westminster Hall, we witness the arrival of a foreign Duke in his splendid coach, 'all red velvet covered with gold lace and drawn by six barbes and attended by twenty pages very rich in clothes'. We go with Pepys, too, to a lecture and dinner at Chyrurgeons' Hall; the guests drink the King's health out of a gilt cup with bells hanging at it (given by Henry VIII to the Company); and every man shakes the cup, to ring the bells, after he has drunk. Few of us would know anything of this delightful ceremony unless Pepys had told us.

Inevitably our last picture of Pepys is as he sits by candlelight, writing his diary. But he has decided, very sadly, that he can keep it no longer, as his eyes are so painful that he fears he will go blind. And thus we must leave him, closing the pages regretfully. But yet we remember many small things about him—that sometimes he wore a 'muffe', that he loved casting up his accounts and counting his money, that he would go from one church to another 'hearing a bit here and a bit there', that he carried a hare's foot as a preservative against the colic. And most of all, we remember his kindness to his old father; often he admitted that his heart was full of love for him. This was a very tender side of Pepys.

Samuel Johnson

1709–1784

'LIFE is a pill which cannot be swallowed without gilding', said Dr Johnson, and although this remark was not intended to be profound, it illustrates one significant aspect of the man. For although he was a brilliant scholar with a marvellous mind he hated being alone. Company, whether frivolous or otherwise, was the breath of life to him. Indeed, he declared that solitude was dangerous, even to the wise and old.

He was, in fact, something of a hypochondriac, and to sit alone in his dreary room induced the gloomy thoughts which he could not face. The truth was he had a morbid fear of death. 'I am afraid', he said, 'I may be one of those who shall be damned.'

He lived, of course, at a time when the prospect of eternal damnation was emphasised in thundering tones every Sunday from the pulpit; parsons felt it their solemn duty to warn their parishioners of what was in store for the wicked and ungodly, unless they mended their ways. And to certain individuals this horrible fear became so real that it poisoned existence; it made 'diversion' imperative.

But this dread of loneliness was a boon to society, for it kept Dr Johnson in perpetual circulation. He was always dining out, and most people were utterly fascinated by his sagacity, his immense scholarship and his brilliant conversational powers. Others, however, actively disliked him. Indeed, if he had had to rely on his looks and manners for popularity he might as well have shot himself, for his huge, uncouth, stooping figure and his scarred and disfigured face were far from prepossessing. He was blind in one eye, his grimaces were painful to watch, and when he walked he

DR. JOHNSON

struggled along like a man in fetters. Fanny Burney declared that his whole person was in a state of perpetual motion.

His looks were not redeemed, either, by fine clothes, as he was extremely slovenly, and wore, as a rule, a suit of rusty brown, old slippers, a shabby wig—always either too large or too small—and black worsted stockings. He wore no ruffles to his shirt (this was unpardonable in such an elegant age), and the knees of his breeches were continually hanging loose. 'I have no passion for clean linen', he once remarked, and apparently he had no passion, either, for washing his hands!

Nor could his manners redeem him, for he laughed noisily— 'like a rhinoceros'—he was arrogant and sometimes supercilious, he was tactless, opinionated, easily offended, impetuous and irritable. As he talked he would whistle under his breath, blow out his cheeks and click with his tongue. And when he was feeling despondent or melancholy he would sigh and groan, talk to himself, and walk from room to room. 'My dear, why do you wear such a vile cap?' he asked a young lady, at a party. 'I'll change it, sir,' said the poor girl. 'Aye, do,' he said. His remarks after being entertained were not always tactful, either. 'This was a good dinner enough to be sure,' he would say, 'but it was not a dinner to *ask* a man to.'

He had a passion for good food. And why not, he demanded?

Some people have a foolish way of not minding, or pretend-ing not to mind what they eat. For my part I mind my belly very studiously, and very carefully, for I look upon it that he who does not mind his belly will hardly mind anything else.

He also said, 'When a man is invited to dinner he is *disappointed* if he does not get something good.'

It is clear, therefore, that Johnson did not shine because of 'the graces'. So what was the secret of his fame and social success? He was neither rich nor well-born, and even his literary work had very little of the divine spark in it; it was merely extremely good journalism. Yet there can be no doubt that Johnson was regarded as a great man. At every party he was soon surrounded by an admiring crowd, all listening breathlessly to what he had to say.

He had an immense personality, and his conversation was so rich, so animated, so forcible, so witty and so wise that it completely fascinated his listeners. That big, deep voice, too, was very impressive, and under that rough exterior was the kindest and most benevolent heart.

We see him most clearly, perhaps, at the home of his great friend, Mrs Thrale, sitting at her immense dining-table as an honoured guest, and partaking of one of her 'noble dinners'. The Thrales were rich, generous and hospitable; they lived in Streatham in lavish style. Mrs Thrale was not beautiful—for she had a bad scar on her lip where her horse had thrown her—but nevertheless she was attractive in a rather vulgar way, with her light blue eyes, fair curls and great vivacity. Her handsome white house was very pleasantly situated in a fine park, and she kept many servants. When she drove out in her coach and four, she would be followed by two servants in a chaise, and two men on horseback. Her hothouses and kitchen gardens were magnificent, and her table was always loaded with pineapples, grapes, melons, peaches, nectarines, etc. She adored celebrities, so for sixteen years a room was set aside for Johnson whenever he cared to stay the night; not however without a little anxiety on Mrs Thrale's part as to what might transpire during the small hours, for Johnson was constantly setting fire to his wig through reading in bed with his head too close to a candle. It was to be hoped that he would not one day burn down the house, with all its valuable contents!

Johnson treated Mrs Thrale with almost paternal gallantry. He confided in her, gave her advice and called her 'my mistress'. She, in return, flattered and amused him; she was naturally witty. 'You care for nothing so you can crack your joke', he declared on one occasion. He also told her that she had all the venom, rattle and attraction of a rattle-snake. Yet if he felt that his teasing had offended her he would say earnestly 'I ask you *pardon*, I ask your *pardon*' again and again. It was he who persuaded her to keep a diary, which was published later. She also wrote bad poetry.

But life had not always been for Johnson a round of 'noble dinners', elegant conversation and gay parties at Ranelagh. For many years he had led a wretched existence in a garret, writing incessantly in order to make a living. At times he had been almost destitute, and had walked the streets many a night when he had not possessed the price of a lodging. He had done translations, satires, criticism, reporting, cataloguing, etc. It was work that was miserably ill-paid. Indeed, he had often cursed the day when he had come to London to seek his fortune. On the other hand, there he had found his level, and he declared that no place cured a man's vanity or arrogance so well as London.

His early youth, too, had been one long humiliation, for although he had been an infant prodigy and a brilliant scholar, yet the years spent at Pembroke College, Oxford, had been wretchedly unhappy; he had been so poor, owing to his father's bankruptcy. He was a proud, melancholy boy, conscious of great powers, and he had hoped to make his way by 'literature and wit', but his poverty, his birth and his looks were all against him. It is not surprising, therefore, that at the age of twenty-six he married a stout and flamboyant lady, the widow of a Birmingham mercer.

Mrs Porter was twenty years his senior, but she had a fortune of £800, and with this limited capital they started a school. Mrs Johnson was apparently a ridiculous figure, fantastic in her dress, affected in her manner, and heavily rouged and painted. After their marriage she treated her husband with some contempt, an attitude which he returned with elaborate deference. For after all, she held the purse-strings.

David Garrick was a pupil at Johnson's school, and to him and his fellow-pupils the Johnsons were merely objects of ridicule. As for the school, for ill or good it lasted only eighteen months.

Mrs Johnson died in 1752, and during the years that followed, fame gradually arrived; every inch of it had been slaved for, and in the year 1762, after his Dictionary had been highly acclaimed (he toiled over it for seven years) he was granted a pension of £300 a year. This was comparative riches, but unfortunately he had numerous dependants, both at home and abroad. He also gave freely to beggars, and he was continually helping literary men in distress. There was Anna Williams, too, the blind daughter of a Welsh physician, whom he allowed to live in his house; she was very poor, and often peevish, but he never lost patience with her. His heart went out, too, to any creature who was ill, however low they might have fallen. He once, therefore, carried a prostitute home on his back; he had found her lying desperately ill in the street. In the shelter of his humble lodging she was allowed to stay until she was well again. He was also particularly indulgent to children and animals, and even in the most bitter weather he would go out to buy oysters for his cat Hodge.

The homage that arrived with the pension was very sweet, for Johnson loved praise, although he was too proud to seek it. And when finally he was asked to go and see the King he was extremely gratified. They conversed in the library for some time, and Johnson declared later that he was the finest gentlemen he had ever seen. Was this contact with royalty, perhaps, the reason why Johnson suddenly burst into splendour and appeared at the theatre one evening in a scarlet waistcoat laced with gold? Certainly the effect was startling, even to his admirers.

But if Johnson enjoyed parties, he also greatly loved drinking and feasting with his literary cronies in a tavern. That is why he was continually forming men's clubs. Friendship meant a great deal to him, and he confessed to Sir Joshua Reynolds that 'if a man does not make new acquaintances as he advances through life he will soon find himself left alone. A man, sir, should keep his friendship *in constant repair*.' At these meetings, Goldsmith, Garrick, Boswell and Sir Joshua were merely a few of those who gathered round him. But Boswell, in particular, regarded Johnson with something approaching adoration.

Boswell, the eldest son of a Whig laird, had a passion for famous people. He hung upon every word that issued from Johnson's lips, and he was so determined to know every detail of the great man's life that he asked the most preposterous and indiscreet questions. But it was impossible to shake him off; the most obvious snub could not penetrate that impervious hide. Boswell's absurd vanity and craving for notoriety, in fact, were ridiculous, and Johnson tolerated him as a sort of impudent schoolboy. Nevertheless he agreed to join him in a tour of Scotland, and Boswell could hardly believe his good fortune. He felt like a dog that had run away with a large piece of meat and is devouring it peacefully in a corner by himself. And here was his opportunity, for almost every word uttered by Johnson was carefully recorded in a book, to emerge later as one of the most complete and interesting 'lives' ever written by any man. It was a work of genius, for Boswell, although inexperienced as a writer, could skilfully set down the very essence of a conversation, the very point of a story, and all that was significant of the great critic and author. Boswell missed nothing, forgot nothing, and apparently falsified nothing.

One of the saddest events in Johnson's life occurred when after the death of her husband Mrs Thrale decided to marry an Italian musician named Piozzi. Johnson was astounded and horrified, for the man was a Catholic. And how could any respectable Englishwoman marry a foreign fiddler? It was degrading, unthinkable, preposterous. Besides, as Johnson was one of Mr Thrale's executors he was intimately concerned with her affairs. How could she do this awful thing?

But Mrs Thrale had no intention of changing her mind, even for Dr Johnson. Piozzi was a man of amiable and honourable character, who was making an independent income from his profession, and there was nothing against him. Besides, was she not entitled to a little happiness? She had married Thrale when she was a young girl; it had been a marriage of convenience. But she had done her duty by him, and had borne him many children, though his conduct had often caused her anxiety and distress. Now she intended to follow her own inclinations.

Johnson was not only horrified but also jealous; there can be little doubt of that. To Mrs Thrale, therefore, he wrote, 'If you have abandoned your children and your religion, God forgive your wickedness. . . . ' It was strong language and hard to forgive, so the friendship came to an end. The Piozzis never returned to England during the remainder of Johnson's life, although Mrs Piozzi was very happy and never had cause to regret her marriage. On her eightieth birthday she was still a vivacious old lady, and gay enough to celebrate her birthday with a ball. She died in the year 1821.

For Johnson now 'the bright day was done'. And it was a mournful thought. Never again would he sit in the handsome blue room at Streatham, talking and laughing; never again would he partake of those rare banquets and that excellent conversation. Gone were the drives and flirtations with Mrs Thrale, and the delightful evenings at Vauxhall, watching the fireworks. Never again would he gorge himself with luscious peaches, and sit talking far into the night while Mrs Thrale poured out interminable cups of tea. It was all over. Streatham had been a second home to him, and he felt very bitter about her marriage.

Yet he clung to life with pathetic tenacity. There was always work; there was always Literature. 'A man *must do something*', he said, for 'the mind stagnates for want of employment, grows morbid and is extinguished like a candle in foul air.' But he had been writing so long, and he had written so much. What more was there to be said, at his age? If only he had learnt to play cards, or had got interested in music. He had, it is true, once bought a flageolet, but could never 'make out a tune'. He had even tried to learn knotting, but without success, though other men had fathomed its mysteries. Where now could he find diversion? Politics bored him to tears, as he felt that they 'meant nothing but the art of rising in the world'. Nor did he care for the theatre. His one venture in play-writing had been painfully unsuccessful; it had failed lamentably.

So as his life drew to a close his old fear of death returned. Was he to be eternally damned? Were there really tormenting devils in hell? He had imbibed the idea with his mother's milk, and he could not, with all his common sense, eradicate it. So when he was ill, as was inevitable from time to time, he would implore his friends to pray for him. 'Remember me in your prayers', he said to Fanny Burney earnestly, and there were tears in his eyes. He himself prayed for hours at a time: 'Have mercy upon me, oh God, have mercy upon me; years and infirmities oppress me, terror and anxiety beset me . . .' He was determined, also, to make his peace with God, even in his will. 'In the name of God, amen . . .', he began. 'I bequeath to God a soul poluted by many sins, but I hope purified by Jesus Christ . . .' What more could he do? If he was to be damned there was no help for it.

There was, however, no lack of personal courage in this remarkable man, and he had never feared pain. In his youth he had boxed and wrestled with the strongest men, and he would part huge fighting dogs, climb trees, run races, swim in dangerous pools, and even ride to hounds, poor horseman though he was. He walked the dark streets unarmed, even in the dead of night when thieves and cut-throats lurked in every doorway. No, it was not pain that he feared.

His book, *The Lives of the Poets*, published in 1779 and 1781 (ten volumes), was the child of his old age, and a work of infinite labour. He regarded it as a responsible task, for his judgement carried more weight than any other man's at that time, and his criticisms were taken very seriously. He wrote, as was the fashion of the time, rather pompously; yet the work was an admirable performance, in spite of its many inaccuracies and some grave defects. He was, for instance, blind to much of the beauty of poetry, for he himself had little feeling for beauty, and any work of a pastoral nature meant nothing to him. He had no ear for music, either, so could not appreciate the charm of a lovely cadence or a subtle rhythm. These were serious 'blind spots' in a critic, but apparently he was quite unaware of them. He judged poetry merely from a moral point of view, as one would a treatise, and in so doing he did scant justice to some of the poets of whom he wrote.

Johnson died very peacefully on December 13th, 1784, happy apparently in the knowledge that he was to be buried in Westminster Abbey. The fears of hell fire were over; the rest had come. There was no longer any need for diversion. His library was sold at Christie's for the sum of £247, and many enthusiastic tributes were paid to his memory. Horace Walpole, however, took no part in them; he had no use for the 'absurd bombast' of Dr Johnson, and he refused to subscribe to a memorial because the old man had declared that Gray's poetry was dull. As for Boswell, he was set down by Walpole as a 'jackanapes', a criticism which has some justification.

But we, who at this distance of time can see all round Johnson, realise that he was a great figure. He was certainly one of the shrewdest and most observant men who ever lived, he was a profound scholar and he had a marvellous insight into human nature. In a modern age he would have made a brilliant psychiatrist.

We remember, too, many odd things about him—that when he entered a room he would go straight to the books and pore over them, shelf by shelf; then he would choose a book and begin to read, quite oblivious of the company. We remember that he treated trifles with the neglect they deserve. 'The rain and the sun, the night and the day were the same to him', said Mrs Thrale. 'If you were tired or uneasy or bored he did not expect you to say so, for "Nobody ever talks of such stuff", he said, "except the people who have nothing else to say." '

We remember that he did not like Scotsmen, or to hear a woman preach. 'It is like a dog's walking on his hind legs' he said. 'It is not well done, but you are surprised to find it done at all.' We remember, too, that he loved to be thought well-bred, and that he was conservative and liked old ways. As to Bishop Berkeley's ingenious theory of the non-existence of matter, Johnson would have none of it, and he struck his foot with mighty force against a large stone, 'I refute it *thus*,' he said indignantly.

Horace Walpole

1717–1797

IT was in the year 1747 that the Honourable Horace Walpole bought the cottage called Strawberry Hill, Twickenham, from the proprietress of a celebrated toy-shop. 'A little plaything house', he called it, and almost immediately he began to enlarge it. 'My towers rise, my galleries and cloisters extend', he said. And so the fantastic structure took shape. He had a perfect passion for everything Gothic; therefore there were battlements, a chapel, turrets and towers, castellated walls and even stained glass windows. It might have come out of a child's fairy-story book, and he himself hardly knew why he built it, yet its creation was one of the joys of his life. 'A Gothic church or a convent fills one with romantic dreams', he confessed. And this, of course, explains everything. His pseudo-castle, Strawberry Hill, was the embodiment of his dreams.

The setting was indeed delightful, for the house was by the river, surrounded by 'enamelled meadows with filigree hedges', and from his window he could see the barges go slowly past. He had a charming garden, and here he erected temples and summer-houses, wreathed in roses and honeysuckles; there were lilacs, acacia trees and nightingales. He could even see from his towers at night the rockets shooting up into the dark sky from Ranelagh or Marylebone Gardens. As for society, he knew everyone and went everywhere, for was he not the son of a famous prime minister, Sir Robert Walpole?

But Horace Walpole's absorbing hobby was to collect antique china, books, prints, furniture, carvings, corals, crystals, miniatures, pictures and armour. And as his collection grew, so did his house. It became necessary to add continually another cloister, gallery or tower in which to house his treasures.

Any morning, then, Horace Walpole might have been found in his panelled study cataloguing his books and pictures, or writing; for he was ambitious, too, to shine as an author. Dressed in silk stockings, knee breeches, a brocaded coat and waistcoat, he was an elegant, dandified figure, and though not of commanding presence, for he was short and slight, yet his manners were as perfect as careful training and good breeding could make them. He was a bachelor of thirty when first he came to Strawberry Hill, and there he planned one day to write the history of his own times. Why not? He had been well educated (at Eton and King's College, Cambridge), he had made the grand tour of the Continent, and he had been intimate with the poet Gray, though, alas, they had quarrelled.

But like so many dilettantes who are not professional authors he liked also to create the right atmosphere in which to write. His house, therefore, was as 'medieval' inside as out. There was an oratory, a refectory, a library, a china room, an armoury, a star chamber, a Holbein chamber, a round drawing-room and so on. There were altars, carved saints in niches, and richly painted coats-of-arms everywhere. And to display his treasures was one of his greatest delights. His friends and acquaintances, therefore, came in swarms to see his collection. 'Lord God, Jesus! What a house!' exclaimed my Lady Townshend, as she climbed the stairs, puffing and panting. And, indeed, it was an exhausting business to tour all those rooms. Dukes and Duchesses, Earls and Countesses, Knights and their ladies, antiquarians, poets, authors and artists were continually ringing at the gate of Strawberry Hill, to be shown over. Even the Prince of Wales, one eventful morning, suddenly arrived. Horace was writing, and in his slippers, with his hair about his ears; he had not even dressed properly. But there was no help for it; down he went to receive them, and at the foot of the stairs he knelt to kiss the Prince's hand. His Royal Highness stayed two hours and saw everything. The Duchess of York came too, later on, and Horace put on a silver

HORACE WALPOLE
From the painting by John Giles Eccardt, 1754

waistcoat for the occasion and did the honours in his very best style.

But Walpole also loved entertaining his friends, and sometimes twenty-four people would be invited to dine. He would receive them 'at the gates of the castle', dressed in a fine cravat and wearing a pair of magnificently embroidered gloves which had belonged to King James I. A splendid dinner would be served in the refectory, to the accompaniment of french horns and clarionets, and the gallery would be illuminated with a mass of candles. The gentlemen, very fine in their rich brocaded coats, and the ladies in their rustling silk dresses, would play at loo and whist until midnight, when a cold supper would be served. Then if the evening was warm and fine they would go out on to the terrace, to smell the new mown hay and listen to the divine nightingales.

Walpole had the entrée to that London society which would go to any lengths in order to amuse itself. At Ranelagh there were Venetian masquerades, in which even the King, the Duke and Princesses took part, though they were of course disguised. They and their friends dressed themselves as huntsmen and peasants, and danced round the maypole; there was music and love-making under the romantic orange-trees, there were masses of flowers everywhere and splendid fireworks. When one of the pavilions caught fire and was burnt down no one cared; it was a mad, hilarious time. And when frolics at Ranelagh and Vauxhall palled there were card parties. Walpole and his friends played interminably. On one occasion, however, having been asked to play with the Royal Duke, Walpole was so anxious to oblige that he threw his hat upon the marble table and broke four pieces of a very fine crystal chandelier; it was a sad humiliation for one so trained in all the graces.

But this amusing life had to be shared, and so to his friends, especially those abroad, he wrote long, long letters. He was a brilliant and witty correspondent, and news of the ups and downs of politics was much appreciated; the gossip of the fashionable world, too, filled many pages.

It is to Walpole, therefore, that we owe this lively picture of the eighteenth century. History was being made, too; there was the war in Flanders, there were battles against the French, and rebellions; there was the trial of the rebel lords and their execution. Horace loved airing his views, and he did it thoroughly; with all the contempt of youth for age he spared no one; he tore his victims to pieces. Often he was extremely malicious and invariably cynical. Yet of one thing there can be no doubt; he was utterly loyal to his friends, and those whom he loved could do no wrong.

As a confirmed bachelor, of course, he had a dog (Rosette) and a cat (Selima). Selima met her death by falling into a china tub filled with goldfish, a sad affair that inspired an ode from one of his friends. He began to be annoyed, too—as a fussy bachelor should—by the noise made by his neighbours. There was one in particular, an attorney's wife, who lived 'at the great corner house yonder' and was 'much given to the bottle'. She was terrified of thieves, and would make the servants fire minute guns out of the garret windows. Extremely annoying! On the other hand, perhaps she was justified, for highwaymen were active everywhere, and Walpole himself was robbed one night in Hyde Park, narrowly escaping with his life, for the highwayman's pistol grazed his cheek and stunned him. After that he always carried a blunderbuss after dark.

Yet Walpole was not really scared. When there was an earthquake—a violent vibration and a great roaring—with bells ringing in several houses and people rushing out into the streets, he was merely amused. The next day, as the long procession of coaches went past his windows taking people out of the town, and he saw others walking in the fields all night, or sitting in their coaches till daybreak, he chuckled to himself. It was barely credible (he said), but some women had made themselves warm 'earthquake gowns' in which they could sit out all night if necessary.

It becomes plain, indeed, that one of Walpole's great qualities was courage, for soon he discovered that he had inherited that most painful of all afflictions, gout. Sometimes he was ill for months and could hardly move hand or foot; and the bouts came with alarming frequency. He lived very abstemiously, he never coddled himself, and yet he suffered horribly. But he bore everything with great fortitude. 'I am ashamed whenever I am peevish, and recollect that I have fire, and servants to help me', he said. Tenderly they lifted him across the room and carried him from table to couch. And there he worked on, writing, cataloguing, reading. Several of his books were published and were successful. And always, even as he lay in agony, he was making plans; there were pictures and treasures to be sold at Christie's; he would go and see them when he was well, and buy what he could. He intended to set up a printing press, too, and print his own works.

There was a suggestion in 1770 that he should be appointed Ambassador to Paris, a city he knew well, and in which he had many friends. There was the celebrated Madame du Deffand to whom he wrote every week. He knew, in fact, the very cream of Parisian society, but to be Ambassador was another matter. Had not his father served his country nobly and then been cast aside? He remembered, too, though without bitterness now, how he himself had been courted and fêted while his father was in power and then dropped after the fall; only his own personality had found him a place in society again. No, he was too old and his health too uncertain for such a task. So he turned it down.

But if there was any bitterness or cynicism left in Walpole at middle-age, it faded as the years passed. He mellowed delightfully, and to his friends and relatives he was both generous and devoted. He even offered half his fortune to General Conway when that distinguished soldier was deprived of his posts. Walpole was intensely proud and fond, too, of his lovely nieces. He took the greatest interest in their engagements and marriages (one of them married a Prince of the blood royal); he drank tea with them, he asked them to dine, he gave them generous presents. It is clear, in fact, that they took the place of the children he might have had.

When old age crept upon him he accepted it with grace and humour. His dreams of fame had faded, but he did not care. 'I look on fame now as the idlest of all visions', he said and, as for himself, he felt that he was so insignificant in the scheme of things that he would 'go out, like a lamp in an illumination that cannot be missed'. But England, he declared (in 1779), was 'lost' and distracted. 'It sinks every day', he said, 'and yet its extravagance and dissipation rather augment than subside. . . . We are like the Israelites that capered round the golden calf.' Courts too, no longer interested him. 'It requires all the giddy insensibility of youth not to be struck with such farces', he said. It was 'so foolish a pantomime'.

The truth is he had lost touch with his age; everything had changed—fashions in dress and manners, and ways of thinking and speaking; even the taste in wit and beauty had altered. 'I have outlived the glory of my family and country', he said, 'yet in truth I think myself very happy.' As for politics, he could no longer take part, 'for when boys are on the stage, a veteran makes but an awkward figure'.

It is sad to remember one other great sorrow of his old age. His nephew, the Earl of Orford, died, leaving the family mansion and estate of Houghton in a condition of utter desolation. He had been a thorn in the flesh for many years and had finally had attacks of insanity. At his death, in 1791, Walpole inherited both title and estate, and it was necessary to arrange for the sale and dismantling of all that remained. A most melancholy task! For Walpole found nothing but a ruin; the glorious house was completely dilapidated and in some parts open to the weather. The woods had become forests, nettles and brambles in the park and grounds were shoulder high, horses had been turned into the garden, 'banditti' lodged in every cottage, every farm had been let for half its value, and much of the land had been sold. In addition, the estate was loaded with debt and mortgages. It was useless to attempt to retrieve anything; the whole place was worthless. Walpole himself knew little of business and felt too old to learn, yet ahead of him were lawsuits and endless conversations with lawyers; as for the empty title, it was merely an encumbrance.

It was a sad day when most of the pictures at Houghton were

sold; large pictures were thrown away, and whole-length Van-
dykes went for a song. A Jew and a grocer bought some of the
pictures; most of the others went to the Empress of Russia, and
were taken away to that country. Walpole bore it all like a true
philosopher. But before his life closed there was one delightful
friendship which brought immense comfort to his old age; he met
two sisters, the Misses Berry, to whom he became quite devoted.
He called them his 'dear wives', and one cannot read his letters
to them, when they went abroad, without sadness, for old age is
very pathetic. It became torture to him even to wait for a letter.
'Our wishes and views were given us to gild the dream of life,' he
had said. The dream was nearly over and the gold was fading
fast. Alas, he was only too aware of it. 'There is no keeping off age
by sticking roses and sweet peas in one's hair', he said. And he
added, 'What am I but a poor old skeleton tottering towards the
grave, and conscious of ten thousand weaknesses, follies and
worse.'

Walpole died on 2nd March, 1797, at his town house in
Berkeley Square; he was in his eightieth year. And with him ended
an era that was in many ways unique, an age that he has described
so brilliantly and fully that we shall always be in his debt. There is
a charm and liveliness in his letters which bring the man himself
vividly before us. We stand by his elbow, in that panelled room,
and see the smile come creeping to his lips and eyes as the quill
scratches over the paper; we hear him chuckling to himself at
some *bon mot* of George Selwyn's, the famous wit. And as we look
over his shoulder and read what he is writing, we smile too, for
the very human way in which his strong prejudices come bursting
out. Then we remember how violent were his likes and dislikes;
he either loved or hated; he could not help himself.

We know him, in fact, at the end of the letters, far better than
he knows himself, for we who are the onlookers see most of the
game. Yet it is a portrait of which no man might be ashamed. The
youthful prejudices and critical superciliousness in the early letters
do occasionally leave an unpleasant taste in the mouth, but in a
man of such discrimination and high intelligence, it is forgivable.

Indeed, unless he had been able to discriminate at that age he would never have come to a right sense of values in his old age; and this he certainly did. He learnt how to live, and his days to the end were filled with creative interests; he was never bored.

And so we come to his books, where it is clear that he can lay no great claim to posterity. Yet at least he had no illusions about the matter. 'A page in a great author humbles me to the dust', he said. What could be more honest than this? No, it is his letters which will live, for here is the picture of an age and the story of a life, drawn with grace, humour and originality. He was a snob, of course; he loved rank and the most fashionable set, the best society; it was his world. But his courage, his loyalty, and his devotion to his friends were wholly admirable.

William Cowper

1731–1800

IT was in the year 1767 that the poet Cowper, accompanied by the newly widowed Mrs Unwin, moved from Huntingdon to Olney, a small village in Buckinghamshire. They had found a house, 'Orchard Side', which though damp, dark and dilapidated was at least within their slender means; but Olney itself was an 'abominably dirty' village, where old women sat making lace in their doorways from dawn till dusk. Men were hanged for theft in Olney occasionally, but otherwise, as Cowper said, occurrences were as 'rare as cucumbers at Christmas'. Cowper was thirty-six, and Mrs Unwin was six years his senior, but she was apparently a remarkable woman, for she 'had a very uncommon understanding', she was a great reader, and she was 'more polite than a duchess'. She and her husband, before the poor man had been flung from his horse and killed, had treated Cowper with great kindness, and he was deeply grateful.

This move to Olney, indeed, is significant, for it is here that Cowper emerges into the full light of day—a curious figure, prim, shy, nervous and puritanical, yet strangely interesting and lovable. He has painted his own portrait through his letters, and has revealed to us also, though quite unconsciously, the reason for the awful tragedy of his life. His whole existence was poisoned by false ideas about right and wrong and a deadly fear of hell. He was gifted, humorous, intelligent and of quick artistic perception, yet he moved through life under the burden of an intolerable despair. In his unhappiness he began to write poetry; this was his refuge, his green valley. And the result is a collection of verse which though of a minor order, we turn to when we wish to read something simple, elegant, pastoral and undisturbing. But it is the tragic figure of the man himself who interests us most.

Cowper's meeting with Mrs Unwin had come like an answer to his prayer, for at that time he had just emerged from a severe ordeal; he had been shut away from the world for two years, having lost his reason. Now he had recovered, and his one desire was to live very quietly. Mary Unwin, with her beautiful auburn hair and her cheerful smiling countenance was not only an attractive woman but a very good woman. She looked upon him as a son, and it was she who now arranged the peaceful pattern of his days. After breakfast every morning they read scripture or sermons together, then went to church, then parted to walk or read. After dinner they talked on religious topics or sang hymns together; then again they walked if it was fine. In the evening Mrs Unwin would play upon the harpsichord (while the little dog howled in anguish under the chair), and the day ended with more hymns and family prayers.

Cowper had his hobbies, too—drawing, carpentry, the making of bird-cages, and gardening. He 'rang a peal every day upon the dumb-bells', and in his small greenhouse, where the windows were well screened with garden mats, for privacy, he liked to sit and scribble. He wrote hymns. Only when the village boys threw mud at the windows or scattered fireworks did he look up. Then indeed he would threaten them with a horsewhip. He was convinced that they did these things deliberately to annoy him.

From his window facing the street there was much to interest him—the arrival of the coach, the postman with his 'tanging horn', the brown-faced gypsies, the labourers strolling into the inn, the squire's lady riding past on her well-bred horse. Sometimes he watched them with a heavy heart, but when spring came, and the 'grass was bespangled with dewdrops', and the birds sang in the old apple trees, his spirits lifted a little. What was the cause of this melancholy, which he hid beneath a merry and joking exterior? There were many reasons: It was depressing to be so badly off (for 'a man cannot always live upon sheep's head and liver and lights, like the lions in the tower') and it was hard to have to live

76

WILLIAM COWPER
From the engraving by Caroline Watson,
after a portrait in crayons by Romney, 1792

in an old cottage that was so very dilapidated; it was almost falling down. He was an orphan, too, and his only serious love affair had come to a tragic end, for his marriage to his cousin Theodora Ashley Cooper had been sternly forbidden; that, indeed, had left its mark.

There were compensations, of course. He had several good friends, and his cousin Theodora and her sister Lady Hesketh were extremely kind. They were continually sending him presents— a handsome desk, a pocket-book, a watch-chain, a beautiful tortoiseshell snuff-box, an almanac of red morocco. They gave him a table, a bed, stationery, an everlasting pencil, the tea and chocolate which he drank, and a purse containing £25. Sometimes, too, a friend would send him a fine barrel of oysters, a salmon, or a pot of pickled scallops. There can be no doubt that his friends and relatives sympathised with his condition. For he had not always lived in this way. He was well born and well connected, but had come down in the world; he could not face the responsibility of any post, so had to rely entirely on a very small income. But he had his pride, so he liked to be well dressed. He wore a fine underwaistcoat of green satin, a smart, well-cocked fashionable hat, a good periwig and a handsome stock-buckle, although it is true it was only a second-hand one, a fact which pained him a little.

Yet life was really very perplexing. He had, for instance, a queer, secret desire for fame, for 'fame begets favour', he said, and 'one talent . . . will procure a man more friends than a thousand virtues'. Yet the thought of publicity was a nightmare to him. He liked, also, elegant, genteel society and the gaiety and vivacity of women, yet a tea-party terrified him, and the thought of love and all that it implied was insupportable.

It was best, therefore, to live quietly in Olney with Mrs Unwin, who understood all his fears. And so they did, for about six years; it was a placid, uneventful existence. Then suddenly, no one knows why, a terrible thing happened; one awful night in February 1773, a dreadful voice announced to him in a dream that he was an outcast and damned for ever; there could never be any hope for him. The experience shook him to the very depths of his being, and, as might be expected, his reason gave way again. What real or imaginary sin he had committed we do not know, but we know from his letters that he considered it an unpardonable one.

His illness lasted for three years, and on his recovery, at Mrs Unwin's suggestion, he began to write poetry; it was a new interest that proved of the greatest value. In his youth he had written love poems, and one of his ancestors was the famous Donne, whose works, of course, he had read many times. That flood of dark, passionate poetry had shocked him a little, for from such a revelation of hidden desires he shrank instinctively, yet there was no doubt of its brilliance and originality. He himself wrote very differently; he needed an escape from his thoughts; he therefore created a world that ran as pleasantly and calmly as a stream through a green meadow. In these peaceful pastures the tumult in his soul subsided; it was a world where sin and its wages did not exist. As for inspiration, it could be found even in Olney; there were sounds and sights all about him—the evening bells, the flower-starred fields, the nibbling sheep, the waggons rumbling along the street, the ploughmen turning up the brown earth. Olney was no beauty spot, but it had its rustic charm, and even a jackdaw could set him versifying:

> Thrice happy bird, I too have seen
> Much of the vanities of men;
> And sick of having seen 'em,
> Would cheerfully these limbs resign
> For such a pair of wings as thine
> And such a head between 'em.

This was clever, and he was not displeased with it. It had, he thought, a ring of originality.

Strangely enough, often he wrote most merrily when he felt most sad. He had his views, too, on the morals of the times. He considered his own 'a vicious age' and he did not hesitate to say so. He strongly disapproved, for instance, of chess, cards and dancing. The popular passion for Handel he denounced as 'idolatry', and as for that 'crowd of voluptuaries who have no ears but for music, no eyes but for splendour and no tongue but for impertinence and folly . . . this is madness', he declared. Above all, there was Brighton, that place of luxury and idleness, where visitors sometimes bathed 'without the decent use of a machine'. Could folly and impropriety go further than this?

It was principally in the greenhouse that he wrote his poetry, and as he sat there one summer afternoon his interest was suddenly roused by two ladies on the opposite side of the road. One of them he knew, but the other was a stranger. She was 'arch and sprightly', with dark hair and soft dark eyes; she had a brilliant smile. Mrs Unwin was willing, so the two ladies were asked to tea.

Lady Austin (for that was the name of the lady with the beautiful eyes) proved even more charming on acquaintance. She was well read, she had travelled, she had a town house in Queen Anne Street, and when she talked she laughed a great deal and was an excellent conversationalist. 'Yet', said Cowper, 'with all that gaiety she is a great thinker.'

It was a friendship that flourished exceedingly, and soon Lady Austin had taken a house in Olney, very close to 'Orchard Side'. Cowper would call there every morning for a chat, and on alternate days they dined at each other's houses. Then doors were inserted in their garden walls, for convenience, and meals were taken outdoors in delightful rustic fashion. A board laid over a wheelbarrow served for a table, and the robin came boldly forward to peck the crumbs. Occasionally, too, the charming new friend would come to 'Orchard Side' to play battledore and shuttlecock, and in a wet season, when the floods were out, she would hire a donkey so that she could visit them. Then after supper, in the summer dusk, Cowper would read aloud to the two ladies, or wind wool for them. He was kindly and attentive, a delightful companion indeed except when a fit of melancholy laid a cloud upon him.

Then, alas, there were two quarrels (for Lady Austin was offended at something Cowper wrote), yet the breach was soon healed, and Lady Austin sent him three pairs of ruffles. But as time went on it became plain that her interest in him was changing.

He and she had corresponded, when she returned to town, as brother and sister—by arrangement—but apparently she now wished to be more than that; her letters embarrassed him. So kindly but firmly he told her so. Indeed, how could a man who thought he was eternally damned share his life with a woman? Marriage was not merely a matter of battledore and shuttlecock, or dining on a wheelbarrow; its implications frankly terrified him. And Mrs Unwin, it is quite clear, agreed with all he said. She, too, was certain that marriage was not for him.

Lady Austin was mortally offended, of course, and came no more to Olney. The correspondence ceased, and life for Cowper resumed its old placid course; the bright interlude was over. He was inevitably a little sad, but, as he confessed to a friend, he and Mary had found the vivacity a trifle overpowering at times; they were better alone.

Cowper was fifty when he published his first volume of poems, but their popularity with the public brought him some measure of happiness. He worked hard on a translation of Homer, too, and wrote a great deal. But life did not continue to flow smoothly, for in the year 1791 Mary Unwin became paralysed and remained so until she died five years later. She had been his rock, his guiding star, his only standby, and after her death life became 'an insipid wilderness'. 'The cliff is here of a height that it is terrible to look down from', he wrote to Lady Hesketh, 'and yesterday evening, by moonlight, I passed sometimes within a foot of the edge of it.' He seriously contemplated suicide, but, alas, had not the courage. Would he not be precipitating himself into that hell, that burning fire, that place of tormenting devils? Suicide, in the eyes of God, was a crime. Or so he had been taught. 'I have no expectation that I shall ever see you more', he wrote, and he added: 'If even death itself should be of the number (of events) he is no friend of mine. . . . Nature revives again, but a soul once slain lives no more . . . Farewell for ever.'

There is no doubt that life had become an intolerable burden, but death was equally painful to contemplate, for he had no hope of salvation even beyond the grave. 'My thoughts are like loose and dry sand', he wrote. 'Adieu!' Even the weather was against him, for although the month was June there were frosty mornings, the walled fruit trees had almost all been cut off, and he was shivering with cold in the greenhouse.

He died on 25th April, 1800, four years after Mary Unwin, and one can only hope and believe that he found peace at last.

And so his poetry and his letters remain. Both are interesting, but his poetry chiefly as an example of what may be written as an escape from tormenting thoughts. It is simple, homely, and often delightful. It is the poetry of human affections, natural, frank, spontaneous, unaffected. It reminds one of a summer's evening in the country, when the sun is setting over the fields and the soft shadows are lengthening. For, indeed, there is no moving force of passion here. He was so out of touch with the real world that there was nothing to inspire him. There are therefore very few lines which linger in the memory, yet there are some which we read again with real pleasure:

> How soft the music of those village bells
> Falling at intervals upon the ear
> In cadence sweet. .   .

And for one beautiful poem, in particular, we shall always be grateful. It stands out from the rest of his work like a diamond picked from a heap of cool stones.

> The poplars are felled; farewell to the shade
> And the whispering sound of the cool colonnade.

Nothing more felicitous has ever been written than these two lines. The rest of the poem however—charming though it is—falls away; for it is too long to preserve its lyricism. As for Cowper's influence on poetry, it was he who set the example of the simple nature verse which was to find such an able exponent in Wordsworth. Cowper's 'message', however, is far from attractive. His narrow creed, his puritanism, his censoriousness, betray a sad lack of intellectual stature. It is useless, in fact, to read Cowper for his message, and he himself, were he alive to-day, would probably deplore much of what he wrote.

As for his letters, although they throw little light on the social scene of the day, for he was never intimate with any of his famous or learned contemporaries, yet they do throw a very vivid light on a pathetic figure. Psychologically, Cowper is deeply interesting, for here is an example of what the Christian religion meant to one man. He had an utterly wrong conception of Christ's teaching, and this had destroyed him. Had he lived three hundred years before he might have been a monk and found immense happiness in that vocation. As a dissenter-puritan he was a most unhappy man, yet he, apparently, was merely one of thousands. The doctrine of eternal damnation had crushed him.

Parson Woodforde

1740–1803

IT is a strange thought that a man should keep a diary merely for his own private purposes and yet as a result produce something which is probably immortal. For here we are, more than two hundred years later, reading with deep interest the daily doings of a country parson in the eighteenth century. Here is a vivid picture of the past, yet it is safe to say that it was never intended to be anything of the sort. And if we ask ourselves why a man in those days kept a diary it was because it was the fashion. Men were urged by their fathers to do so as a religious exercise. They would be told to set down their meditations, their struggles with sin and their triumphs over the flesh. These things mattered in those days, for the devil was always at one's elbow.

But many men found that a daily recital of their spiritual ups and downs was a little depressing. On reading the diary over, the 'sins' appeared so lamentable that the hope of heaven seemed to fade. On the other hand, the record of what one had for dinner each day, and the account of that pleasant party up at the squire's was extremely interesting to look back on. That could be recorded with safety and pleasure. And when one had grown old and long in the tooth, one could read all this back, and say to oneself: 'We had merry doings in those days. I could drink and dance with the best of them. I could ride, and run, and make love. I was not always an old man, gouty, shrivelled and tottery . . . Yes, I have had my day.' And as one fingered the old diaries and read the faded writing, everything would be bathed in a warm nostalgic light. The picture had acquired the mellowness and luminosity of an old master; it was entwined with lovely dreams. Indeed, did ever birds sing so sweetly as in one's youth? Was ever grass so green, and dew so sparkling, and moonlight so silvery? Did not the stars shine more brightly in those days. And were not women more beautiful . . . ?

But we who read the old diaries to-day also catch something of that golden glow and that luminosity. For there was a colour, a simplicity and a richness about those old days which made the events stand out sharply and clearly.

Parson Woodforde, of Weston Longeville, Norfolk, sat down almost every day for forty-three years to write up his diary. He did not attempt to lay bare his soul, for as a parson that might have been extremely unwise; the diary might fall into the wrong hands. It was best to record, in fact, just as much as would not bring discredit on oneself. And so he did.

James Woodforde, then, was one of those amiable, friendly parsons, of whom but for his diary we should never have heard. He was handsome, with a benign expression and large thoughtful eyes: He wore an elegant white wig, as was the fashion, and his wigs were carefully dressed twice a week by his manservant. James Woodforde was, in fact, the sort of good-looking parson whom any young woman might have been glad to marry; yet he was a bachelor, and his niece Nancy kept house for him. Their lives flowed as smoothly as a stream through a meadow, for they were far removed from 'the world's great strife'. The Seven Years' War, the War of American Independence, and the war set alight by the French Revolution, blazed and smouldered to ashes without producing even a thin haze of smoke in their lives; such was their rustic isolation. It is true that there were some rumblings of the outer world. There had been great village rejoicings on the taking of Quebec; there were also fireworks and bonfires when a King was crowned, and on the Queen's birthday one of the parson's servants would mark the event by firing a blunderbuss three times.

Yet on the whole, life in the country was uneventful, though there were some pleasant diversions. A dinner-party followed by a game of cards in the best parlour was delightful, and to go coursing with one's greyhounds was a fine recreation. Sometimes

REV. JAMES WOODFORDE
From the painting by Samuel Woodforde

the parson rode to Norwich, too, attended by his manservant on horseback, and if one met an acquaintance on the road he doffed his hat with a flourish and said, 'Good morrow to you, sir!', and one replied, with one's best bow, 'Your servant, sir!' It was a world where elegant manners counted. Ladies curtseyed continually, and men bowed. They bowed very low to their superiors (of whom there were a few) and very stiffly to those slightly beneath them (of whom there were many); men were always bowing.

Yet for a country parson there were also duties which one did not really care about. James Woodforde was very tender-hearted, and when he was obliged to perform a 'forced' marriage ceremony it went against the grain. The reluctant bridegroom had been brought to church handcuffed so that he could not escape. As for the parishioners, the parson was called so constantly to their bedsides to perform the last sad rites that it became a part of the pattern. Yet he was always a little upset by the experience. When he found an old man 'totally senseless with rattlings in his throat' James Woodforde invariably made a note of it in his diary. But the next entry, even without a pause, would read: 'Dinner to-day boiled beef and rabbit roasted.' For men, of course, were bound to die, but the world must go on. and one must eat while one could.

The amount of food, in fact, consumed by James Woodforde and his niece Nancy is almost incredible. The ducks, geese, turkeys, fish, oysters, legs of lamb, pork and beef, etc. would have fed a family four times the size. But food *mattered*. When one went out to dinner, too, one expected a good spread. There would be many courses, each more succulent than the last, and sometimes a dessert of twenty dishes. As for the wine, rum, brandy, beer and ale, etc., that was consumed, it almost defied comprehension. The parson himself, although considered an abstemious man, drank a pint of port every day, in addition to his regular wine and ale. He brewed his own ale, and apparently it was very good; his neighbours always praised it. The local blacksmith was also something of a smuggler, and on certain dark nights he would arrive at the parsonage with various mysterious barrels, which of course had to be bottled without loss of time.

There was a great deal of entertaining, and the parson and his niece dined out regularly with friends, in rotation. After dinner they would play quadrille or whist; there was much visiting, too, and sometimes Woodforde and Nancy would go with a party into Norwich for a few days. They would go to the theatre, attend an elegant ball, or a grand concert. His own village, Weston Longeville, was a very small one, with a population of about 360, and Nancy sometimes complained that life was dull. This made him a little uneasy, yet he did his best. Almost every year they paid a long visit to their relatives in Somerset, driving by coach, and staying a few days in London on the way, to see the sights. They went to the Tower to see the lions, and to the Mansion House. This long journey was a tremendous undertaking and a great adventure, what with the highwaymen and the bad roads, etc., and when they returned to Weston Longeville safe and sound James Woodforde never forgot to thank God fervently for his 'great goodness' in preserving them from so many dangers.

Parson Woodforde kept five or six servants, and he owned a cow called Polly, a pig or two, two or three greyhounds, and two or three horses. He 'bled' his horses himself ('two quarts each'), and made up their medicines. He bred very fine fish in his ponds, he made his own hay, and he grew a little barley. This was not farming; he was merely self-supporting. His servants, on the whole, were excellent, for he never engaged any who were not experienced and well recommended; nevertheless, they were but human, and several useful maids were obliged to leave because they were discovered to be 'with child'. Often they stoutly denied this fact, but there came a time when it could no longer be hidden. Menservants, too, often seemed to promise well, but after a few years became 'saucy', or took to the bottle, or fell in love with one of the maids. One extremely useful man, indeed, caused a great upheaval one day by beating the maids in the kitchen until they screamed for mercy; he then proceeded to jump into the pond. And all this, apparently, for unreciprocated love.

Love, in fact, would not be denied, even in the country, and Parson Woodforde himself had had his dream. When he was a young man in Somerset he had fallen in love with a certain sweet-tempered Betsy White, and he had decided to 'make a bold stroke' and ask her to marry him. She was apparently quite willing, but time passed, the parson was in no hurry, and Betsy went to Devonshire, where she met another man—who was worth £500 a year—and married him. It was a sad blow, and 'She has proved herself to me a mere jilt' wrote the parson in his diary. Since then he had admired young women at a distance, and when a pretty girl, all gaiety and frills, came to the parsonage (she was generally a friend of Nancy's) and he noticed the rustle of her silken skirts, he was a little overwhelmed. He loved the vivacity of youth, yet marriage was quite another matter, and as time passed the idea receded further into the background.

He was fond of children, too, and on St Valentine's day about fifty rosy-cheeked cottage children would come to his door. To each one he would smilingly give a penny. Mr and Mrs Custance, who lived in 'the big house', were constantly adding to their family, and as each baby arrived Parson Woodforde would be asked to go to the house to christen it. But before he left he would be given a carefully folded piece of notepaper in which reposed the sum of five guineas. Five guineas was a large sum in those days. But Mr Custance was 'the squire'.

The squire and his wife were so very kind; they were always inviting the parson and Nancy to dinner. They would send their coach for them, and at the party there would be much grand company. After dinner Mrs Custance would play the Sticcardo Pastorale (a glass musical instrument) very softly and prettily. The squire himself called at the parsonage several times a week, and rarely came empty-handed. A servant behind would bring a brace of pheasants or a basket of delicious fruit. Mr Custance would stay talking for perhaps an hour, and would drink a glass of wine before he went. Sometimes Mrs Custance would make a morning call, too, with her little boys and their nurse; and Parson Woodforde would give to each boy a humming top, or something of that kind.

On the other hand, sometimes the great people dining at the

Custances were a little stiff towards the parson and his niece, and James Woodforde would write in his diary on his return 'One must confess that being with our equals is much more agreeable!' The Custances were greatly beloved in the village, and when Mrs Custance was ill in bed for some months after childbirth, there was much concern on every side, and little else was talked of. But finally when she had recovered sufficiently to 'come downstairs' it was an occasion to celebrate, and guns were fired, the church bells rang a merry peal, and Parson Woodforde gave his servants a bottle of gin to drink.

It must not be supposed that the parson had not sown his wild oats, for, indeed, as an undergraduate at Oxford he had been a very gay spark. He had danced a great deal, and could take his part gracefully in a minuet; he had been to bear-baitings, played 'crickett', given bachelor supper parties, and played fives against the church wall with his cronies. He and his friends used to drink hard, and the frolics that resulted were not always to his credit. Often they were extremely noisy and abusive, and on one occasion Woodforde had been turned out of bed and 'locked out of the room, naked'. Once he threw some wine in an undergraduate's face, a frolic that cost him a bottle of wine. On a later occasion—whether drunk or sober is not recorded—he went into Court to hear some prisoners tried, and to secure a good seat he jumped from two men's shoulders, 'leapt upon the heads of several men', and then scrambled into the prisoners' 'place'. The judge warned him sharply that he could not stay there, and he was reprimanded for the noise he was making. He was apparently cured of his heavy drinking, however, by receiving a bad head wound after a drunken fall, and he made a vow never to be drunk again. It was a necessary lesson which proved extremely effective.

His undergraduate days, in fact, were pleasant to recall. He had learnt to play on the spinet, and his dear mamma had bought the instrument for him as a present. He had always been well dressed, and had chosen his clothes and wigs with great care. When the King died he had ordered a very fashionable suit of mourning (it was essential), and later on he had gone into 'second mourning'. But that was only temporary. Soon he had been able to blossom out into the brocades and fine waistcoats that every eighteenth century gentleman wore; the silk stockings were essential, the lace cravat had to be immaculate, the ruffles of fine lace, the shoebuckles as handsome as possible, and the hat fashionable and well-cocked.

He remembered, too, how he had exchanged snuff-boxes with a girl friend, 'by way of remembrance', and sometimes as a present he had given a girl a pair of pretty garters. He had been to merry sheep-shearing parties, fancy dress balls, and indulged in country dancing. When he had first become a curate he had been 'rung into the parish', and he remembered how merrily the bells had pealed. He remembered, too, how he had risen at two in the morning in those days to write a sermon for a funeral. He had been young and enthusiastic then.

Yet this life at Weston Longeville was not unpleasant. The tranquil procession of the seasons always brought something of interest. A new horse and chaise, too, was an exciting event, and an election made conversation for weeks; a new piece of furniture caused quite a stir, and when his new sideboard and a large mahogany cellarette arrived, it was pointed out to friends that it had been brought all the way from Norwich by two men and carried on their backs. That was surely a feat of strength and endurance.

Nancy's new gowns of flowered taffetta trimmed with satin ribbons were also an event, and when the pig produced a large healthy litter one felt that there was little wrong with the world. As for funerals, they were great social gatherings, especially if they were 'handsomely conducted' and 'in the best manner'. A great deal of wine was drunk, and all the servants would be given mourning hatbands and gloves. Christmas was a festive time, and Christmas day itself was marked by a generous dinner which he gave every year to about twenty old men of the village. They came up to the parsonage in high glee, and had an uproarious party.

But there were nasty jolts now and then. One of his greyhounds, for instance, escaped, without a thought for the consequences, and ate a whole shoulder of mutton belonging to a friend. For this she was hanged the same night, for dogs could not be allowed to commit crimes of that kind. Why, only the other day a gypsy had been hanged for robbing a girl of 2s. If men were treated thus —and that was the law—animals could not hope to escape punishment either. But Brother Jack, who lived with him for a time, was a great trial. He kept such 'mean company', was always 'busy with the girls', and was continually coming home drunk. Then he would 'make a riot', swear like a trooper, and behave like a madman. Time and again he was so drunk that he fell off his horse and was brought home bruised and battered. But John was incorrigible. Talking and scolding were useless, and finally he had to be told that he could no longer live at the Parsonage. He had had many chances, but his behaviour was too outrageous.

As for the thunder-storms, in those days they were positively terrifying, for the lightning conductor had not been invented, and church steeples were frequently struck. Houses, too, were often struck by lightning and burnt down when the thatch caught fire. In a bad storm, thatches would be stripped off the rafters, windmills would be blown down, and tiles sent flying across the fields. When the wind blew in that alarming way the parson sat up all night; it was unwise to go to sleep.

The winters, too, as the years passed, seemed to become more severe. Perhaps he felt them more keenly because he suffered from gout. And how it snowed in that part of the world! When first it fell it was beautiful, and the countryside was turned into a glittering fairyland. But soon lanes were piled so high with snow that only the tops of the hedges could be seen, villages were cut off, sheep were buried, the cattle could find little to eat, and no food supplies could come through. The milk froze in the pans, the water in the basins was thick with ice, and poor men and women were frozen to death on the roads. Often it was almost impossible to get to church, yet one must struggle there somehow and preach a sermon, although the congregation would be a very small one. Not even the squire and his family would come.

As for the parsonage, which with its thatch looked so cosy, probably there was something wrong with the house, for the cold in winter was really intense, yet he was determined not to coddle himself. 'We have not had our beds warmed nor do we intend to' he said in his diary, yet at the same time he was shaking and shivering all day; there seemed to be a pain at his heart, he ached all over with cold, and in his miserable bed he could not sleep for shivering. The cottagers, too, suffered bitterly at this time, so money was collected for them all through the parish, for coal and bread. Winter was a terrible season for the poor, and he and the squire gave generously.

But spring would come at last, and the first swallow (he made a note of it), and the crocuses and daffodils. The birds sang again, the corn was green, the lambs skipped in the fields. Again he was able to go coursing with his greyhounds, and they would kill a lusty hare. He would prune his roses and walk round his apple trees to see whether the blossom had set. Then from the copse would come the call of the cuckoo. In a very few weeks the raspberries and strawberries would be ripe, and there would be hay-making. And then followed autumn, with its luscious fruits—walnuts, and apples, plums, apricots and pears. He was famous for his apples and apricots. Indeed, God was good. One must thank him daily for his infinite mercy and his many blessings. The parson was, in fact, constantly amazed at The Almighty's varied creations, and when he saw a peacock spread its tail he remarked in his diary: 'How wonderful are thy works, O God, in every being!'

Did James Woodforde, perhaps, ever regret being unmarried? Certainly he was lonely when Nancy went away for a few days to stay with her friend Betsy Davy. There was no one to play cribbage and backgammon with in the evenings. And when Betsy and her odious young man came to stay, and the three of them whispered together in corners and kept him utterly in the dark about their affairs he felt so very sad and alone. Betsy's young man was gay, lively and extremely good company, yet there was something a little odd about him, and finally it transpired that he was very heavily in debt to almost every tradesman in the district. He had proved himself to be an incorrigible liar, too. But a year or so later, at the age of twenty-one, he died of consumption.

Parson Woodforde was not at all surprised, and he had never liked or trusted the fellow, so there was no more to be said.

Another matter which bothered James Woodforde occasionally was when Nancy was 'saucy', though perhaps that, too, was natural. Perhaps at times she even envied the maids who were 'with child'. Possibly she would have liked a home of her own and some pretty babes in her lap. Yet apparently it was not to be, for she stayed on, arranging his dinner-parties, bottling his fruit, and supervising the baking and 'washing'. The latter operation was quite an affair, as they washed only once in five weeks, and it took four days for the washerwomen to complete the task and finish the ironing. Nancy was a good housekeeper and he had no fault to find with her.

So the years passed, and the pattern of life changed very little; the gout came more frequently, the winters were a plague, and for some reason his health declined. Dr Thorne came and gave advice, but James Woodforde did not improve, and soon he was quite unable to take the service in church; the task had to be delegated to his curate. This was very sad, and James Woodforde missed his parishioners; he missed gazing out over that sea of familiar faces on Sunday morning, and the friendly greetings at the church door after service. They would all enquire so kindly after his health; they were fond of him. But he had already had one fainting fit in church, and often he felt very weak and ill; sometimes he trembled all day and his legs would barely support him.

Yet he did not forget his diary; it had become a habit, and he continued to record his doings. But on October 17th (1802) which was a Sunday, he made the last entry:

> Very weak this morning, scarce able to put on my Cloaths and with great difficulty, get down Stairs with help. Mr Dade read Prayers & Preached this Morning at Weston Church. Nancy at Church. Mr & Mrs Custance & Lady Bacon at Church. Dinner to-day Rost Beef, etc.

The diary had come to an end, and on New Year's Day, 1803, James Woodforde died. He had completed his picture of the eighteenth century, and in doing so he had painted his own portrait. Peace be to his ashes.

As for Nancy, after her uncle's death everything in the house was sold—the books, the pictures, the plate, the furniture, and her uncle's clothes. The poultry, the cows, pigs, horses, chaise, greyhounds, etc., were also disposed of, along with the hay, corn and carts. The auction was a dismal affair. But Nancy's great friend, Mrs Bodham, was with her, and a few days later the squire's daughters came to fetch Nancy to stay with them for a time. Then finally she went back to Somerset to live. From there she often wrote to the Custances, and they too remembered her with kindness. The little boys who had often walked with their mamma to the parsonage were now fine upstanding young men; they took snuff and were men of the world. But sometimes, when they sat in church listening to the sermon, they remembered a former parson who with a kindly smile had given them humming tops. They remembered, too, his beautiful model ship, all complete with sails and rigging, etc., which on special occasions would be dressed out and put on his 'lagoon'. They remembered how bravely the sails filled and how splendidly the ship tacked when the rudder was properly set. . . . Sometimes in that lake the parson would catch a pike weighing as much as seven pounds. An immense fish! They remembered, too, that when the parson had a stye on his eye he would rub it with his tom cat's tail; this was supposed to be a cure, but it never worked. The parson had believed, also, that when the cat washed over both her ears there would be a change in the weather, and he had told them that once when he was in London the mob had hooted and hissed the King as he passed in his coach, and had finally broken the windows . . . But all this was a long time ago, for already Parson Woodforde's tombstone was looking a little weatherworn.

William Blake

1757–1827

IN that fine portrait gallery of English literary men born in the
latter half of the eighteenth century the strange, vigorous,
fantastic figure of William Blake stands out as clearly as if
clothed in the bright light of his own visions. He wandered
amongst 'the stars of God' and he was 'under the direction of
messengers from Heaven, daily and nightly'. This visionary world,
in fact, was far more real to him than the world of reality, and he
pursued it with passionate devotion. Indeed, we come to the
conclusion that had he been born a few centuries earlier he would
probably have become a monk, for he was truly pious, and his
singleness of heart indicates that the life would have suited him
admirably.

But Blake's father was a strong dissenter (a fact which
moulded his whole life) so the idea of a monastic vocation probably
never entered his head. Instead, those tremendous visions were
translated into poetry and pictures. The Bible, which exerted a
powerful influence on his mind, provided him with a huge myth-
ology of his own—a world of angels, disciples, Adam and
Eve, serpents, the fires of hell, the stars of heaven. But when
this forest of symbols became dark and confused (as often happened) terror would enter into his soul; some awful calamity
was impending. Was it the Last Judgement? We strongly suspect so, for that indeed was an important part of the belief of a
dissenter.

Yet when Blake emerges from this confusion—and he does so
most often in his poetry—we step out into the fresh and tender
world of babes, angels, children, flowers, fairies, trees, valleys

WILLIAM BLAKE
From the painting by Thomas Phillips, R.A., 1807

and mountains; there is the lamb, the lily and the rose, and these objects shine and glow; they are transfigured. Here is the voice of Blake that charms and delights, the voice that knows little of worldly matters or even of deep contemplation; it is the wisdom of childhood, as fresh, spontaneous, innocent and inconsequent as the song of a bird, and equally melodious.

That Blake was a strange child is beyond dispute, for even at four years of age he insisted that God had 'put his head in the window' and made him scream with fright. Later on, at eight, he announced that he had seen a tree filled with angels, a statement for which his father threatened to beat him.

The boy was, in fact, so sensitive and highly strung that he was never sent to school, but was encouraged to learn drawing instead; casts were provided for him and he was also given money with which to buy prints and engravings. Eventually he was sent to Pars' Drawing School where he learnt to draw from antique casts, and finally he was apprenticed to an engraver.

Blake was good to look upon, with his fair, luxuriant, curling hair, wide forehead, fine eyes and large head; the expression of his face was both cheerful and dignified, and although he had a snub nose it merely added to his benign appearance. 'I have always thought', he said, 'that Jesus Christ was a snubby and I should not have worshipped him if I had thought he had been one of those long, spindle-nosed rascals.' In stature Blake was short, but he was strong, well-made and broad-shouldered; there was about him an air of intense, tremendous vitality and he held his opinions fiercely. Religion, of course, was the subject on which he felt most strongly. That anyone should deny the existence of hell, for instance, or cast doubt upon his visions, enraged him, and, indeed, he quarrelled so violently and continually with his fellow-apprentices that he was sent out a great deal to make drawings at Westminster Abbey. Here he might have been seen almost any day of the week, drawing swiftly and with eagerness the tombs, the carved angels, the groups on the screen, the brasses, the gargoyles and Last Judgements. The magnificent atmosphere of the place awed and inspired him, for here was a world of solemn beauty dedicated to that religion which had so wrapped itself about his soul.

One evening, while working in the Abbey, he had a vision of Christ and the Apostles. Is it surprising, therefore, that he resented any interruption of his celestial thoughts? So when an inquisitive Westminster schoolboy intruded he flung him angrily from the scaffolding and then laid a complaint before the Dean. But when it grew too dark to draw, and the sun set with a burning glitter upon the Thames, he would wander in the dusk, seeking to quench his thirst for beauty. The stars that hung brightly above the dark water, and the moon that rose above the masts and sails of the anchored ships, had a strange fascination for him. The children that lingered by the river bank delighted him too and he was never tired of writing about them:

> Twas on a holy Thursday, their innocent faces clean,
> The children walking two and two, in red, and blue and green;
> Grey-headed beadles walked before, with wands as white as snow,
> Till into the high dome of Paul's they like Thames water flow.
>
> O what a multitude they seemed, these flowers of London town.
> Seated in companies they sit, with radiance all their own.
> The hum of multitudes was there, but multitudes of lambs,
> Thousands of little boys and girls raising their innocent hands. . . .

But how their childish troubles saddened him! He could not contemplate without emotion a lost child, a weeping babe, a lonely orphan, a wretched chimney-sweep. Alas, there were only too many unhappy children in his day; they swarmed through London in ragged and miserable bands, homeless, unwanted, uncared for. It was not unusual to see a tiny illegitimate infant left on the roadside to die, while passers-by merely shrugged their shoulders and looked the other way. But in the country, somehow, the children seemed happier:

> When the voices of children are heard on the green
> And laughing is heard on the hill,
> My heart is at rest within my breast,
> And everything else is still.
> 'Then come home, my children, the sun is gone down,

And the dews of night arise;
Come, come, leave off play, and let us away
Till the morning appears in the skies.'

'No, no, let us play, for it is yet day,
And we cannot go to sleep;
Besides, in the sky the little birds fly,
And the hills are all covered with sheep.'
'Well, well, go and play till the light fades away,
And then go home to bed.'
The little ones leaped, and shouted and laughed,
And all the hills echoed.

Was it the thought of children, we wonder, which set his mind on marriage and made him choose a bride after a very short acquaintance? Catharine was a graceful, dark-haired girl, the daughter of a market-gardener and quite illiterate. They were married in 1782 and she was a wonderful wife, being an excellent housekeeper and 'rigid, punctual, firm, precise'. She believed implicitly in all his visions and addressed him always as 'Mr Blake'; he spoke of her as his 'beloved', and in one of his letters he calls her 'my dear and too careful and over-joyous woman'. He taught her to read, to write, to draw and to help him in the printing and colouring of his engravings. She refused to keep a servant, not only for reasons of economy but because 'no servant could be scrupulous enough to satisfy her'. And how calmly she fell in with all his wishes, even to sitting naked beside him in the garden, under an arbour, so that they might represent Adam and Eve. That at least is the story, and we are told that they were reading *Paradise Lost*.

But could one be surprised at anything Blake did? The world of reality had no meaning for him. He was merely concerned with the urgent task of setting down in either pictures or poetry, his visionary world. 'I am really drunk with intellectual vision whenever I take a pencil or graver into my hands', he said, and he added, 'Nothing can withstand the fury of my course among the stars of God and in the abysses of the accuser'.

How we envy him his journeys among the constellations! But there were also the fierce elements of life to be reckoned with—

fire, lightning, the sun: the whirlwind, tigers, lions, snakes, scorpions, the flaming swords, etc. They haunted him·night and day and were always breaking in where surely they were out of place, for he had an ear that was exquisitely tuned for the delicate phrase and the felicitous word; a suggestion of violence might bring down the whole edifice. Yet therein lay his triumph, for he was able to blend fierceness and delicacy almost magically in his poems, and in doing so create that essential effect in lyric poetry— the element of strange surprise. A word or an image suddenly blazes forth; it is unexpected and yet the only word, the only image. It lights up the poem, it throws upon it that enchanting 'light that never was on land or sea'.

'Let us be crowned with roses', said Hafiz. 'Let us drink wine and break up the tiresome old roof of heaven into new forms.' Blake, we feel, was always striving to crown us with roses, to break up the roof of heaven. He would probably indeed have become almost oriental in his poetry but for that early Puritan or Dissenter influence. This, however, is what he wrote:

> Tiger, tiger, burning bright
> In the forests of the night;
> What immortal hand or eye
> Could frame thy fearful symmetry? . . .

Surely this came red-hot from the brain! And who but Blake could have written it? It owes nothing to any man or to any age; it is the outcome of either a vision or a nightmare.

But what of the patient dark-haired Catharine? Could she accompany him on these fantastic journeys? Unfortunately no. But she understood him perfectly; she accepted without question all his strange assertions—that his poems were written without premeditation and sometimes even against his will, as 'the authors were in eternity'. He told her that on the death of his brother Robert his soul 'rose through the ceiling, clapping its hands for joy', and that this same Robert continued to send instructions for methods of engraving, even after death. She endeavoured to take part in her husband's visions, too, and on winter nights they would both stare into the fire and draw what they saw there. Also, when he would rise in the night, agitated and almost distraught, to write down what was 'dictated' to him she would rise too and sit beside him, silent and motionless, sometimes for hours. Her presence calmed and steadied him; he came to rely on her. She accompanied him too when he walked out into the country, sometimes for whole summer days and far into the night. Only when he suggested that he should add a concubine to his domestic establishment—in the Old Testament manner—did she hang her head and weep. He therefore abandoned the idea.

> Let us agree to give up love
> And root up the infernal grove . . .

he wrote in one poem. But whether this applied to his concubine we do not know. Yet it is so finely said that the answer seems unimportant. Love, in fact, played a very small part in Blake's life; there were so many other activities, engraving and illustrating, and printing and binding; even the inks and colours were made by his own hands, and his print shop in Broad street was always a hive of industry. But he did not make a fortune, nor did the public hail him as a mighty genius. He gave drawing lessons, however, to pupils of aristocratic families (they delighted in his odd conversations) and he was offered the post of drawing master to the Royal Family (which he refused). But his friendships went sadly awry, for was ever man so quarrelsome? There was William Hayley, who greatly admired his work and invited him to go and live at Felpham, where Blake was to start 'a new life'. Indeed, at first Blake was delighted with his cottage by the sea, where 'voices of celestial inhabitants are more distinctly heard'; visions came to him there readily, and he saw them walk on the shore, 'majestic shadows, grey but luminous, and superior to the common height of men'. This was far removed from reality, and when his fantasies carried him 'into a land of abstraction where spectres of the dead wander' he was mortally afraid. There was work to do, however, and he began to decorate Hayley's new library with the heads of eighteen personages—Hayley's illegitimate son and the poets

Milton, Homer, Ercilla, Ariosto and Spenser, etc. It was fascinating work, but Hayley made 'imbecile suggestions' and they quarrelled, not once but many times. There was that extremely unpleasant affair, too, which resulted in a prosecution for high treason. Blake was tried, but defended himself with great ability and was acquitted, the verdict being loudly cheered. Finally he returned to London, declaring that at Felpham he had spent 'the darkest years that ever mortal suffered'.

But if reality was unacceptable, and fantasies were terrifying, what was left? One could live neither in this world nor the next. His friendships had failed too. Nothing remained therefore but a bid for fame, so he decided to hold an exhibition in London of his most important pictures. This surely would establish his reputation. It did nothing of the sort, however; and *The Examiner* referred to him as 'an unfortunate lunatic whose personal inoffensiveness secures him from confinement'. It was a terrible criticism; it was unpardonable. But was it justified? All that can be said is that Southey (who saw him a few years later) decided that 'His madness was too evident, too fearful'.

Blake was writing at this time a poem called 'Jerusalem; The Emanation of the Giant Albion', and there can be little doubt that the poem was clear to him, but to his public it was difficult, cryptic and highly involved. Indeed, it could only be surmised that those heavenly messengers who dictated to him were using a new technique.

This strange poet was, in fact, rapidly becoming more absorbed in his own fantastic world. Yet at the same time the trend of intellectual thought in his contemporaries was increasingly turning towards the new facts of science, facts which threw grave doubts on some of Blake's most cherished beliefs. Was this to be borne? Was this profanity to be listened to, even for a moment? No, he would have none of it, so during some discussion on the vastness of space he cried out in a thunderous rage, 'It is false! I walked the other evening to the end of the heath and touched the sky with my finger.' What could one say to such a man? His hearers could only look at each other in silence and change the subject.

But Blake was not to be deterred, and he decided to put the thing into verse for all to read:

> Mock on, mock on, Voltaire, Rousseau,
> Mock on, mock on, 'tis all in vain.
> You throw the sand against the wind
> And the wind blows it back again. . . .
>
> . . . . . .
>
> The atoms of Democritus
> And Newton's particles of light
> Are sands upon the Red Sea shore
> Where Israel's tents do shine so bright.

Yes, glory be to God, nothing could shake his simple faith.

Blake's old age was happier than might be supposed, for although apparently he suffered for a time from persecution mania, yet he achieved some measure of peace. Crabb Robinson paid him many visits and found him 'pale, with a Socratic countenance and an expression of great sweetness . . .'. He was quiet, self-possessed and modest, and when he spoke of his visions it was in the ordinary unemphatic tone which belongs to trivial matters. He declared, however, that he had committed many murders, that the Supreme Being was liable to error, that he had had conversations with Socrates and Jesus, and that Milton had warned him not to be misled by the mistakes in *Paradise Lost*. 'I have been very near the gates of death', he said, 'and have returned very weak and an old man, feeble and tottering, but not in spirit and life, not in the real man, the imagination, which liveth for ever. In that I am stronger and stronger, as this foolish body decays.'

He had, indeed, no fear of death, but his wife declared that she had 'very little of his company; he is always in Paradise'. Blake had his admirers at this time, too—a group of young men who thought him a prophet, and regarded his house as almost holy; 'The House of the Interpreter' they called it. There was also his friend Linnell who gave him many commissions and was infinitely kind; at his house in Hampstead Blake was certain of a warm welcome.

But the day came when Blake needed no more commissions; he died at Fountain Court on 12th August, 1827, and his death was

a triumphant one. He died singing Hallelujahs and songs of joy.
'He made the rafters ring', says Tatham. He was buried in London,
and his grave, being a common one, was used again and the bones
scattered. Can we regret this last indignity? It would be foolish to
do so, for Blake himself attached little significance to the body. He
who conversed with paradise, dined with the prophets Ezekiel
and Isaiah, and had visions of angels, could afford not to care.

Blake never received during his life the recognition due to him,
but there can be no doubt that he has received it since. Those
exquisite lyrics, 'The Echoing Green', 'To the evening star', 'To
the Muses' and 'The Tiger' are set securely in the crown of
English literature. They glow with as bright a light as any Elizabethan lyric, for beauty is arrested, held suspended and stamped
for ever in these poems. There are, it is true, things less happy,
which are unworthy of his genius, for some of his poems do not
soar as a lyric should; they stumble along the ground like a
wounded bird. Yet all his poems are intensely revealing, for Blake
could hide nothing; taken one with another they tell the story of
his life and character. His joys, his angers, his loves, his desires,
his visions, his terrors; all are there.

But while we admire Blake for his innocence, his simplicity, his
unworldliness and his love of children, he is not really an attractive
figure. There is something repelling about the violence of his
anger, his quarrelsomeness and his immoderate abuse of the artists
whose work he did not like. His critics were 'a nest of villains',
and he was unforgiving, almost vindictive.

> In the morning, glad I see
> My foe outstretched beneath the tree. . . .

We are bound to reject too his declarations that 'The tigers of
wrath are wiser than the horses of instruction' and 'Whoever
believes in Nature disbelieves in God, for Nature is the work of
the devil.'

Yet there are certain pictures of Blake which linger in the mind.
We remember how he once found a fairy on a streaked tulip and
brought him home, how he used to sing his own songs to his own

music, and how on a cold winter's night, when he had been visiting at Hampstead, Mrs Linnell would send him home wrapped in a shawl, for he was old and frail. We can see him so plainly, accompanied by a servant carrying a lantern to light him across the dark heath. We should like to hold out a hand to him too when he was

> Walking along the darkened valley
> With silent melancholy. . . .

That Blake was mad at times there can be little doubt, but there is a divine madness—a release from the ordinary ways of men— which nature can afford to produce once in a while. He was at least sane enough to inspire other men with a belief in his genius, and although his prophecies and visions are not likely to change the history of mankind, yet they show how far man may divest himself of worldliness, how pure in heart he may become. They show that education can never be a substitute for vision, nor even a necessary adjunct to the translation of that vision. And although most of us have no hope of seeing a tree filled with angels, or God riding on the whirlwind, or the morning stars singing together, yet we cannot but envy Blake a world so rich and strange.

Samuel Taylor Coleridge

1772–1834

W HY, we ask, is it so easy to picture Coleridge? Why, as we dip into his poetry and ponder on his life, does the man rise up before us so clearly? A fine glow surrounds him and it will not be dimmed.

It is all very strange, for in many ways he was a poor creature. He was weak-willed, vain, moody, sentimental, indolent, untruthful and hopelessly unpractical; as a philosopher he cuts very little ice, as a husband and father he was a failure, and one dare not assert with a loud voice that he was a really great poet. Yet he was much loved and immensely admired. Charles Lamb and Dorothy Wordsworth worshipped him, and Hazlitt once walked ten miles through the mud merely to hear him preach. His voice rose, we are told, 'like a steam of rich, distilled perfume', and according to Leigh Hunt 'he could persuade a deist that he was a Christian and an atheist that he believed in God'.

It is plain, then, that what makes Coleridge stand out so clearly is his extraordinary personality. It was said of him that he 'talked like an angel' and that he could almost hypnotise an audience with his amazing eloquence. Also, he was by nature ardent, guileless, generous, affectionate and utterly charming. Charles Lamb declared that 'the neighbourhood of such a man was as exciting as the presence of fifty ordinary persons', and there was no denying 'the rich graciousness and courtesy of his manners'.

But even Coleridge's greatest admirers could not assert that he was handsome, for there was 'a strange wildness in his aspect', and although the black glossy hair, the broad forehead, the fair skin and the large grey eyes were excellent features, yet his mouth

SAMUEL TAYLOR COLERIDGE
From the painting by Thomas Phillips, R.A.

was 'gross, voluptuous, open', and the nose was feeble and insignificant. Also, he was inclined to stoutness, and as he walked he shuffled from one side to the other. He was in fact an odd creature.

But we see Coleridge most clearly, perhaps, in the Lake district, walking the hills and dales with William and Dorothy Wordsworth. The two men were much in sympathy, and would talk poetry and philosophy for hours. Apparently they talked interminably, and Wordsworth's sister Dorothy, who adored them both, would sit listening in rapture. 'Ah, dear friends, even to anguish I love you', declared Coleridge. He always expressed himself extravagantly, but he was sincere. And, indeed, he owed a debt to Wordsworth, for it was he who had inspired so much of his poetry; it was he who constantly urged him to write. At Nether Stowey—'a green and silent spot amid the hills'—'The Ancient Mariner' and 'Christabel' were written. They were composed almost in a state of trance, and there was a wonderful magic about them.

Yet it was Dorothy who really idolised Coleridge. 'May all the stars hang bright above her dwelling', he said. And when he arrived on a visit she would become so agitated that she could barely speak. But soon they were sitting by the fire and he was reading his poems to her. And then they would walk at night in the woods alone (William had gone to bed with a headache). On warm summer nights, too, they would sit talking in the orchard until the stars faded. For time had no meaning for them. Even in winter they walked together by moonlight. They were both enraptured with beauty; and the warm light on the hills, the blazing sunset, the heavenly rainbow shining through the clouds sent them into ecstacies. Every flower was a perpetual wonder, every glow-worm was a marvel, every diamond drop of dew was a revelation. Beauty was their world, their god, their very life.

But these visits, of course, only lasted a short time, and Coleridge would say farewell. It was always a sad farewell, and Dorothy would be left desolate; in the privacy of her room she would weep bitterly. There were letters, of course; she wrote continually. Such long, long letters. And for his in return she would watch the post with anguish. And when the beloved letter came she would thrust it into her bosom with trembling hands. 'A safer place for it', she said. In the meantime every tree and mossy stone which reminded her of him brought tears to her eyes. Where he had carved a name on a crag she kissed each letter. Was ever any woman's love so tender and poignant as hers? She was a middle-aged spinster but she would gladly have died for him.

It was, of course, easy for Dorothy Wordsworth to love such a man. Unlike Mrs Coleridge she was untroubled by debts, children and petty domestic affairs. She was able to sympathise with his 'agonising' letters, for she was not emotionally involved; his debts were no concern of hers. She was free, too, to go with her brother and Coleridge on a tour of Scotland—a heavenly tour. Over hill and dale they wandered, walking day after day, in the Trossachs, utterly enchanted with the scenery. They did not care where they spent the night, or what the weather was. They felt like happy children on a holiday, or gypsies wandering in another world. They slept in barns, and sometimes in cottages where hens roosted in the smoke-blackened rafters above their heads. They met simple rustic folk who might have belonged to the Middle Ages, and beautiful peasant girls who might have turned the heads of princes. The kindness and hospitality they met with was quite touching; the tour was a splendid success. But always, like a golden thread running through the tapestry of their wanderings, there was poetry. They read it to each other continually, they wrote it, they breathed poetry. It was almost a shock to get back to the unkind world where domestic ties counted, where debts were harassing, where one must find the means to live.

Indeed, Dorothy knew only too well how difficult Coleridge had found life. She knew his history. He had been a remarkable boy, and even at Christ's Hospital where he had received his education, he could always command a rapt and admiring audience; at the age of fifteen he was already discoursing on Plotinus, and by the time he became a scholar of Jesus College, Cambridge he had advanced far in the realm of philosophical thought. He was a fine scholar, with an immense comprehension and a wonderful memory. Yet he was a poet, too, and he devised for himself a paradisal dream-world, a world that poets have always inhabited. But when this dream-world faded it left him in black despair, for he was extremely introspective and suffered from nightmares. Such was his youth, so full of promise, and yet from his very nature so ominous.

Soon, indeed, he was drinking too much, had fallen into ways of debauchery and had got into debt. He became, in fact, almost suicidal, and at last, faced with a bill he could not pay, he had enlisted as a private in the 15th Elliott's Light Dragoons. The name he gave was Silas Tomkyn Comberbacke (said to have been borrowed from a shopfront). But not even the dragoons could turn him into a soldier, and after about four months he succeeded in obtaining his discharge. With his shirts worn to rags he had returned to Cambridge.

The next idea that had occurred to him (with the aid of Robert Southey) was to start a colony, on communistic lines, in the backwoods of America. It was to consist of twelve men and twelve women, and a mere £2,000 capital was needed with which to purchase 300 acres of land. 'New life, new hope and new energy' had poured into him at the very thought of this fantastic plan. (Alas, he had no sense of humour!) He even learnt carpentry to prove that he was in earnest. But the first step was to find a woman —one of the twelve—whom he could lead to this elysium, and Southey decided that an acquaintance of his, a Miss Sara Fricker, would be eminently suitable. Coleridge was not in love with Sara Fricker, yet he finally drifted into a marriage with her. It was in 1795 and he was twenty-three at the time.

The 'colony' idea, of course, came to nothing; it was merely the first of many idealistic schemes; for to erect elaborate and elegant castles in the air was one of Coleridge's pastimes. Magazines were started, great epics were planned, huge philosophical treatises were sketched out, and each new enthusiasm completely carried him away. As De Quincey said, 'he wanted better bread than can be made with wheat'. Something was achieved, of course, for he wrote poems and books on philosophy, he gave lectures, he preached sermons. But it was all too spasmodic, and unfortunately so many manuscripts were left unfinished.

Besides, was ever man so beset with worries? In spite of generous gifts and allowances from many friends, debts mysteriously accumulated, and his financial affairs were always in a state of chaos. Sometimes he had not a shilling in his pocket, and the patches on his knees and elbows were a disgrace. As for his domestic life, children simply would be born, his wife had little patience with his amiable futility—she was more concerned with matters of rent, food and clothes for the children—and there was always some love affair to complicate matters.

At Greta Hall, where Sara Coleridge and her children lived with their uncle Southey, a room was always kept ready for Coleridge, but he rarely came. Sara and her children did not like being dependent on Southey, but what could they do? Their father could not keep them. Poor Sara! Our sympathy goes out to her, even at this distance of time, for she was a simple, affectionate homely woman: there was nothing artificial about her, except, indeed, her wig, which was 'as dry and rough and dull as a piece of stubble, and as short and stumpy'. How could she find time to dress her wig fashionably, she who was always at her wits' end for money, and had three children to educate?

As for Coleridge, why were publishers so difficult, and friends so quarrelsome, and relatives so peculiar? He could not understand it. Why, when he failed to turn up to give a lecture, were people angry about it? He came if he could; surely a poet could do no more. His health was bad, too, so who could blame him if he took opium as a relief, and then brandy as a relief from opium? Life was 'too, too fatiguing' and one must get through it as best one could. His genius, it is true, had blossomed, but the question was, would it continue to put forth flowers? There was a morbid languor about him and a fitfulness of purpose that increased as time went on, to the deep concern of his admirers. For the opium was doing its deadly work. His was 'a mighty intellect put upon a sensual body', said Leigh Hunt. . . .

Yes, Dorothy Wordsworth knew all this. But perhaps Coleridge should speak for himself. 'I am much better', he wrote, 'and my new and tender health is all over me like a voluptuous feeling.' Should he not then start to write, to finish those brilliant beginnings? But how could he write poetry to order, or, as he declared, 'with his breast against a thorn?' Besides, was he not a philosopher with a special message? In that direction, surely, lay his genius! Yet his philosophy took little account of the facts of life, for his passionate hunger for the ideal and his search for an absolute beauty would not fit in with the new tendency towards relativity. He could not believe, as Wordsworth did, in that perfect relation between man and nature, and having all his life 'hungered for eternity' he would not admit that what he sought was unattainable.

This, then, was the cause of his intellectual unrest, this passion for something fixed when all was moving. He tried to apprehend the absolute, to set fixed principles in politics, morals and religion, based on one form of faith. He refused to see that life is too complex for any simple remedy, and that one faith can never be the final answer. And it was, of course, the artist in him which created the conflict. He was an artist with a passion for metaphysics. Indeed, he declared that he had been 'driven from life in motion, to life in thought and sensation'. But the real tragedy lay in the fact that neither his faith in nature or Christ was strong enough to make him face up squarely to life. As an artist and a philosopher he wanted to run with the hare and hunt with the hounds. He was not the first to try, but his attempt was doomed to failure.

It was in Germany, in company with the Wordsworths, that he hoped, possibly, to find some answer to his problems, and here he met the learned and the noble. They flattered and praised him, and he went to the Harz mountains with a party of students, where they slept on straw in village inns; it was all very primitive and stimulating. Back to the simple life, in fact. Later on he decided to go to Sicily, for which journey Wordsworth and Sir George Beaumont each advanced him £100 towards his expenses. In Malta he secured what might have proved an interesting post, but he was unhappy there, his health did not improve, and the opium habit began to take its toll of him; his will began to fail, and he shrank from pain or labour in any form. Finally he returned to London, ill, penniless and 'worse than homeless'. 'I feel with an intensity unfathomable by words my utter nothingness, impotence and worthlessness in and for myself', he said. It was a tragic cry of despair.

There were, of course, his children. There was Hartley, 'the visionary boy', whom Coleridge likened to the moon among thin clouds moving in a circle of his own light. Alas, although he too was talented and a poet he did not acquit himself well at Oxford, and was finally deprived of his fellowship, owing to intemperance.

But Coleridge also had a daughter, Sara. She was a lovely, delicate, large-eyed child. 'Send me the very feel of her sweet flesh, the very look and motion of that mouth—O, I could drive myself mad about her', he wrote, when she was a baby. He adored her, he told her fairy tales and gave her a candle when she was afraid of the dark (remembering his own nightmares). She grew into a beautiful woman and he insisted that she should be finely dressed. He could not offer her a home, yet she worked untiringly for him, editing, verifying, copying, making notes (she spoke six languages). But was she embarrassed, we wonder, at the christening of her first child, when Coleridge—cheered, we suspect, by the good christening wine—spoke for six hours without stopping?

Indeed, he who 'launched into his subject like an eagle dallying with the wind' could not be silent. But gifted though he was, his lectures—and he gave a great many—were not always successful, for sometimes he arrived in the lecture room in a state of exhaustion, almost of coma, and some of his lectures were a little strange. When it was advertised that he would lecture on *Romeo and Juliet* he began with a defence on school flogging, and after touching on the characters of Elizabeth and James I (as compared with Charles) he went on to discuss wit and fancy, languages, poetic diction and Shakespeare and purity. Many of these lectures were, of course, very fine in themselves, but his friends could not fail to notice 'the wild eye, the sallow countenance, the tottery step, the trembling hands, the disordered frame'.

There is no doubt that the man was lovable, for De Quincey—they were not even old friends—made him a gift of £300, others helped to support his family and educate his children, and even Byron, who was merely an acquaintance, sent him a present of £100. (Coleridge had recited 'Kubla Khan' one morning in his lordship's house in Piccadilly—a very fine performance which had greatly impressed the noble lord). In addition, he received several small legacies, and one friend sent him £30 every year to pay for his holiday. It was an act of pure kindness, but nevertheless Coleridge never forgot to remind him if the gift failed to arrive. It is a sad fact, too, that although he often left letters unopened and unanswered for weeks (he did not reply when Southey wrote to consult him about the future of his children), yet he never lacked the courage to write and ask for loans.

As time went on and the opium habit grew, writing became increasingly difficult. He declared that opium gave him repose—'a green spot of fountains and flowers and trees'—but the after-effects—an utter wretchedness of mind and body—were disastrous. In fact he could neither cope with life nor face death, and every year he grew more portly, more uncertain in his step, more talkative. His ideas, too, became strange and exaggerated; he was continually weighing one idea against another. And, heavens, how seriously he took the matter! Thought, apparently, divided itself into ranges of hills, and the highest and most beautiful mountains were only for the very few; he reached out continually to these glittering peaks, wandering from range to further range, with a restless wanderlust that had become a habit.

> My genial spirits fail
> And what can these avail
> To lift the smoth'ring weight from off my breast?
> It were a vain endeavour
> Though I should gaze for ever
> On that green light that lingers in the west;
> I may not hope from outward forms to win
> The passion and the life whose fountains are
> within.

He still saw 'the green light that lingers in the west', but it could not satisfy him, for he was no longer willing to accept beauty; he wished to reduce it to a formula.

It was at this time that his friends, the Morgans, with whom he lived for some years, tried unsuccessfully to break him of the opium habit. Then finally he himself realised that something must be done, and he placed himself in the care of a doctor, a Mr Gillman. For eighteen years he was a member of this household, and he achieved some serenity of mind. His room at Highgate looked upon 'a delicate prospect of wood and meadow with coloured gardens under the window'. Here he cultivated his flowers and fed the birds. With his white hair and a book in his hand he was a benevolent and scholarly figure, and little children loved to talk to him. The circle of his admirers grew, too, and no literary pilgrimage was complete without a visit to Coleridge. He could still talk magnificently, but more often his conversation descended to mere tedious preaching. 'I never hear him talk without feeling ready to worship him, and toss him in a blanket', said Carlyle. Coleridge's philosophy, however, had changed very little, for he was still unable to reconcile his ideas with contemporary facts. The industrial age had started, and the growth of scientific knowledge had thrown a new light on religion and philosophy. It was inevitable. But science meant nothing to Coleridge; he could only lament for the past and resist everything progressive.

It was at this time that he suggested that his friends and admirers should subscribe £200 a year towards his expenses, so that he might be able to write the great books he had in mind. Unfortunately his friends did not respond, for even his most devoted admirers had lost faith in his 'literary air-castles', as his wife called them.

'The archangel' (Coleridge) was by now 'a little damaged' as Charles Lamb put it, but nevertheless he occasionally attended a dance, and at one party even demonstrated his gaiety by throwing a wineglass through a window. He was also to be seen walking on fine days on Hampstead Heath, surrounded by a small circle of admiring disciples.

Coleridge lived to be sixty-one, and having made a last un-successful attempt to throw off opium he died on July 25th, 1834. The wonderful voice was silent at last. For many years he had been afraid of dying in his sleep. All his fears were ended now.

But it is impossible to contemplate the life of Coleridge without sadness, for he was gifted with great powers which never came to full fruition. To leave behind a handful of wonderful poems merely whets the appetite and makes us hungry for more. Coleridge's poems are, of course, no longer fashionable, yet where in modern poetry can one match the rich fancy, the wild, tender, pensive atmosphere which he could create at will? He and his contemporaries used too many words, of course, by the standards of modern taste, yet it was really a question of pace; life was leisurely in those days; there was time for contemplation, for slow reading, for sipping the rare flavour of a fine thought.

As to Coleridge's philosophy, he has been called a failure because he lost himself in abstractions and a false morality. But this was inevitable, because he was first and foremost an artist, a poet, and he was therefore bound to strive after an absolute beauty; that was his impetus. Coleridge has been blamed, too, for 'seeking self-indulgently after beauty'. But this was inevitable, too, for unless the jug is filled there is nothing to pour out. As for the criticism that he was wrong to lose touch with reality, surely an artist is entitled to do this so long as his reason remains sound enough for him to express his vision intelligibly. He may also lose touch with humanity and therefore fail as a man, but that need not prevent him from being a great artist. For greater artists than Coleridge have been willing to sacrifice health, love, friendship and even life itself to genius, in the belief that a man's life is merely a speck in eternity; it is his work that counts, the work he leaves to posterity.

> O Lady, we receive but what we give,
> And in our life alone does nature live;
> Ours is her wedding-garment, ours her shroud!
>   And would we aught behold, of lighter worth,
> Than that inanimate cold world allowed

To the poor loveless ever-anxious crowd,
    Ah, from the soul itself must issue forth
A light, a glory, a fair luminous cloud
    Enveloping the earth—
And from the soul itself must there be sent
    A sweet and potent voice, of its own birth,
Of all sweet sounds the life and element!

Charles Lamb

1775–1834

IN that ancient retreat in London known as The Temple, which lies between the Strand and the river Thames, Charles Lamb, 'the most lovable figure in English literature', spent his childhood, and if what is dear to the heart lives on in the spirit, surely his delightful ghost haunts the place still! It is true that many of the buildings were laid low by the bombing of London, but the plane trees still cast their graceful shadows across the lawns and the flagged alley-ways, and one or two fountains and sun-dials still remain. What good company there is, too, for do not the Knights Templars also haunt the place, the men who with their own hands built the Temple Church in the twelfth century?

But for No. 2, Crown Office Row, where Charles Lamb was born, the poor ghost must search in vain. Gone, too, is the winged horse which stood over the entrance to the Inner Temple Hall, but the carved stone lamb and flag still adorn the ancient door-ways. Even a ghost must get his bearings!

Charles Lamb was the son of a poor scrivener who with his wife and family occupied humble rooms in The Temple, and it is recorded that as the result of a petition to the Governors of Christ's Hospital the young Charles was admitted as a pupil to the school at the age of seven. He was a strange, delicate boy, religious and studious; he stammered 'abominably', he was very small for his age, and he walked in a slow and deliberate manner which was most unusual in a boy. Yet his popularity with both boys and masters was undeniable, for he was witty, gentle and amiable.

In Christ's Hospital life was spartan, and the food was poor and inadequate. If a boy ran away he was brought back and fettered, and for the second offence he was punished by solitary confinement in a tiny, miserable cell, where he was fed on bread and water, and beaten. For the third offence he was thrashed unmercifully before the assembled school, and expelled. This was the type of discipline meted out even to seven-year-olds. Nevertheless, Lamb was not unhappy there and the atmosphere of the place made a deep impression on him. The cloisters, the ancient rooms, the stately dining-room hung round with good pictures; it was all very fine. In his blue gaberdine, yellow stockings and yellow tunic he went his way as thoughtfully as a young monk.

Holidays were spent in the precincts of The Temple, and here we catch a glimpse of him watching with childish awe the Old Benchers walking to and fro on the terrace. Severe and dignified, and wearing their wigs and gowns, they seemed to the young boy almost godlike. But other holidays were spent in visits to a great Elizabethan house, Blakesware, in Hertfordshire, where Lamb's maternal grandmother was housekeeper. She was a wonderful woman, this grandmother, tall, upright, graceful, and the best dancer in the country. She slept alone, without fear, in that huge empty house, as the owners had departed. Lamb was allowed to wander all over the vast rooms, still magnificent with their carving, gilding and fluttering tapestries. There was a marble hall, filled with busts of Emperors, and in the nursery the very battledores and shuttlecocks were still lying about, as if the children had thrown them down and then been spirited away. Indeed, strange things happened at Blakesware, for it was said that an apparition of two infants could be seen gliding up and down the broad staircase.

There is no doubt that this house fired Lamb's imagination, but at fourteen the city claimed him and he became a clerk, finally securing a post at East India House. Here, perched on a very high stool, in a dark, dusty room, he wrote all day in great ledgers, Possibly it was the very monotony of the work which turned his thoughts to books; at any rate, before he reached manhood he had discovered a passionate delight in fine literature. Shakespeare, Sir Thomas Browne, Christopher Marlowe, Ben Jonson, Andrew

CHARLES LAMB
From the painting by William Hazlitt, 1804

Marvell, Sir Philip Sidney, Chaucer, Donne, Spenser, Milton and Jeremy Taylor; these were the authors he loved, and he haunted the book-stalls of London in search of their works. It was thus that his shabby library came into being, many of his books being clumsily patched, by a cobbler. Then to share his enthusiasm for literature was Coleridge. He and Lamb had been schoolfellows, and now they had met again. In the little smoking-room of 'The Salutation and Cat' in Newgate Street they would sup together frequently, and sit talking, chiefly of literature, often far into the night. Coleridge was a magnificent conversationalist.

But at the age of twenty, as the result of a love affair, Lamb lost his reason, and spent some weeks in a madhouse at Hoxton. This insanity, unfortunately, was 'in the family', yet while it lasted, as he confessed to Coleridge later, he had many hours of pure happiness. 'Dream not, Coleridge, of having tasted all the grandeur and wildness of fancy till you have gone mad', he said. The following year, however, brought most tragic evidence of the family taint, for Lamb's sister Mary, overwrought by nursing her mother —who had practically lost the use of her limbs—became mentally deranged and stabbed her mother to the heart. Mary was sent away to an asylum, and on her release Lamb calmly put aside all thoughts of love and marriage and decided to devote the rest of his life to her. Finally, when the family home was broken up he and Mary took rooms together at Mitre Court Buildings. 'She would share life and death, heaven and hell with me', he said. And, indeed, they were very devoted.

This home of theirs consisted of merely two attic rooms, only to be reached by climbing many flights of stairs, but it was there that those informal gatherings of literary men took place. Wordsworth, Coleridge, Southey, Leigh Hunt, Hazlitt, the Burneys, Dyer and Godwin; these are merely a few of the brilliant authors who attended Lamb's parties. 'That bitch Mrs Godwin' (as Lamb called her) was, however, never invited! One did not meet there, as Hazlitt said, the rich and fashionable, but men of brilliant intellect, men who were destined to produce the most lasting influence on the literature and thought of the day. They played whist and talked interminably. How they 'skimmed the cream of criticism!', and it is said that Lamb 'furnished many a text for Coleridge to preach upon'.

There were oyster parties, too, in which the invitations ran thus: 'This night we shall be at home . . . Doors open at five o'clock. Shells forced about nine. Every gentleman smokes or not as he pleases.' Mary Lamb, of course, acted as hostess on these occasions. Dressed in dove-coloured silk and snowy muslin kerchief, she was a delightful addition to the party. She was a good classical scholar, she wrote charming verses and she was one of the most serene and sensible of women.

Lamb soon became a familiar figure wherever he went. 'That is Mr Lamb, the author' it was said, as his short, quaint figure passed down the street. He dressed oddly, like some Quaker, always in black knee breeches and gaiters; he wore a white neckcloth, chinese silk stockings and a very old hat; sometimes he wore a frill to his shirt and a black velvet collar to his coat—a fashion thrust upon him by his tailor. Often, too, he carried a green umbrella. But his peculiarities were quite eclipsed by his charm and good looks. His complexion was clear and brown, the eyes intelligent, thoughtful and of sweet expression, the hair black, crisp and curly. 'It was a head worthy of Aristotle', said Leigh Hunt. And what excellent company Lamb was, too! He had a most sprightly wit and could not enter a room without making a joke. But he was also an excellent scholar, and according to Hazlitt, 'no one ever stammered out such fine, piquant, deep, eloquent things in half a dozen half sentences'.

It is strange, however, that Lamb knew little Latin or Greek, and nothing of modern languages, botany, science, astronomy or geography. He had no ear for music, either, and declared that he had been practising 'God save the King' in secret all his life, yet he had never mastered it; opera was 'inexplicable anguish' to him, and Oratorio reminded him of 'some cold theatre in Hades'. Yet where could one find such excellent good sense and such sympathy, especially for the unfortunate? He was always assisting some poor clerk or struggling author, and would swear that he really had no use for the money himself; it was quite superfluous. It was Lamb and his sister, too, who went in all weathers to visit Leigh Hunt in prison, and it was Lamb who stood by Hazlitt when he was in great disfavour with the rest of the world.

But Lamb could play the fool, also, on occasion, and certainly as a young man he spent one Sunday morning in the stocks, having been involved in a frolic at Barnet. It is also recorded that he once opened his garden gate to a donkey—so that it might feast on his grass—and that when he was asked to take charge of a school class, he solved the problem by simply giving the pupils a whole day's holiday.

Lamb's essays were all written in his spare time. In his study, the walls of which were covered with Hogarth's prints, he spent hours scribbling. He would begin to write an essay and declare gloomily to his sister that he could 'make nothing of it'. Yet in the end it was excellent. Only in one direction did he not succeed —as a playwright—for he wrote a farce, *Mr. H.*, which was quite a failure when produced in London. Lamb, of course was bitterly disappointed, yet he joined in merrily when the audience hissed.

It would not have been surprising at this time if Lamb had blossomed out into a fashionable author, received by the rich and the noble, and entertained in a royal way. But Lamb cared nothing for such things, and a less ambitious man never trod the streets of London; he was quite content with his lot. Besides, there was always the tragedy of his sister's health, for one could never be certain about Mary, and madness would descend upon her with awful regularity, sometimes as often as twice a year. She knew the signs only too well, and when an attack was imminent, she and her brother, both in tears and carrying a strait-jacket, would walk to the asylum, where she would remain until her health was restored.

Lamb suffered intensely at these times, for he too was highly strung, and he too had his depressions—'as black as a smith's beard'. But he kept his sanity, and if sometimes he tried to drown his sorrows by drinking with his friends there is surely every excuse for him.

> I have been laughing, I have been carousing,
> Drinking late, sitting late, with my bosom cronies.

There is, indeed, one record of him being carried home shoulder high, and sometimes, after he and Mary had moved to Islington, for the benefit of her health, it was necessary for his friends to see him home in a coach, for the New River ran close to his house, and in the dark he might have slipped in and no one been any the wiser.

Islington was in the country in those days, and they had found a small white house with a garden, where he could sit under his own vine. But at first he 'fretted like a lion in a net', for he 'had no passion for groves and valleys'. And how he missed the

> 'fine, indifferent pageant of Fleet Street . . . markets, theatres, shops sparkling with pretty faces, lamps lit at night . . . the noise of coaches, the drowsy cry of the mechanic watchman at night . . . Inns of Court with their learned air . . . old book-stalls . . . the sun shining upon houses and pavements, squares where I have sunned myself, my old school. . . .

And was any walk comparable to a walk from St Paul's to Charing Cross? Even beggars (to whom he always gave alms) and chimney-sweeps had their charm for him. He was a cockney through and through.

Nearly thirty-three years of Lamb's life were spent at East India House, and then, after an appeal to his employers, he retired. His salary had by this time risen to a good round sum, and he was therefore given a pension of £450 a year. This retirement was 'like passing from life into eternity' and he declared that he would not have served another ten years for seven hundred thousand pounds. Yet although at first his new freedom delighted him, in time he missed his 'old chains' and the lack of regular occupation. Time seemed to stand still, and he confessed that often he did not know the day of the week, or the month. His sister's attacks, too, grew more frequent and in her absence he was often lonely. It was at this time that he became a great walker, and would cover on an average fourteen miles a day. He would walk from 'The Horseshoe' to the 'Rose and Crown', and then on to 'The Rising Sun'. 'Now I have walked a pint', he would say, and that is how he calculated distances.

There were, of course, other diversions; he often paid visits to Oxford and Cambridge. He loved 'the tall trees of Christ's, the groves of Magdalen', and when in his sober black he was sometimes mistaken for a don it amused him; it was so natural to return the salute with a dignified bow. There was also a visit to Coleridge in the Lake district, where those interminable talks on literature were resumed. We know, of course, who did most of the talking, and in that curious study we can see them so clearly. It was a 'large, antique ill-shaped room' with an old-fashioned organ, 'big enough for a church', but never used. There were shelves of scattered folios, an aeolian harp, and an old sofa. Here Lamb stayed for three weeks, and although he had previously declared that he cared neither for lakes or mountains he was much impressed with the scenery.

The death of Coleridge was a great sorrow, and left an immense gap in Lamb's life, as they had been friends for fifty years; there was no one to take his place. 'All, all are gone, the old familiar faces.' 'What a beautiful autumn morning this is', he wrote 'if it was but with me as in times past when the candle of the Lord shined round me.' However, Lamb lived only a few months longer. He died from erysipelas as the result of a fall.

Wordsworth, as Lamb's great contemporary, was asked to write an epitaph for his tombstone, and thereupon produced 130 lines of poetry, which he suggested should be engraved in two columns! This was the poet who had once declared that he 'did not see much difficulty in writing like Shakespeare if he had a mind to try it', to which Lamb's comment had been, 'It is clear nothing is wanting but the mind'. The epitaph for obvious reasons was not used. As for Mary Lamb, she survived her brother for eleven years and lived to be eighty-two.

As an essayist Charles Lamb shines amongst his contemporaries like a fine star on a dark night. He possessed, in fact, all the qualities that go to make a good essayist—a sure and discriminating taste, the gift of not taking either himself or his subject too seriously, and a style that is at once intimate, eloquent, clear and emphatic, though never didactic. There is no straining after effect, no attempt at unnecessary ornamentation, and neither bitterness nor bias. He never says, like so many essayists, 'I will show you how to think on this subject' (for that, he feels, would be 'a sort of insult to an intelligent reader') yet we realise at once that here is a man with a strong original mind and a great heart, a man who could be companionable even to a tramp. But we feel, too, that this son of a scrivener was intensely human; he had sinned like other men. He got drunk on occasion (two glasses of wine made him almost tipsy), he could be irritable, he could not pack up a trunk or tie a parcel, and occasionally he let his humour go a little too far. Sometimes, too, he made mistakes, even in his judgement of men, for we remember that although he was always most generous in praising the work of his contemporaries he did not understand or appreciate Shelley. 'Shelley, the great atheist, has gone down by water to eternal fire', he said, when Shelley died. This was unworthy of him, but it proves that Lamb had his personal prejudices, to which, of course, he was quite entitled.

His love affairs, too, were quaint and incomprehensible, for he was in love for years with a Quaker girl to whom he had never spoken! 'Every quakeress is a lily,' he said. Yet we understand him perfectly when we read that he tried, over and over again, to give up smoking. Tobacco was his 'sweet enemy' and his 'evening comfort', but it was also his 'morning curse'. 'This very night', he wrote on one occasion, 'I am going to leave off tobacco. Surely there must be some other world in which this unconquerable purpose shall be realised.'

His battle against the habit of snuff-taking enlists our sympathy, too, for we remember how one summer's evening he and his friend Hone, walking on Hampstead Heath, decided firmly never again to take a single pinch, then with great strength of mind threw their snuff-boxes away into the furze and brambles. The next morning, however, the two friends met accidentally on the same spot, and each had to confess that he was searching for the lost snuff-box.

There is no doubt that Lamb made a success of his life, and to speculate on what other work he might have achieved had he been more free is rather a waste of time. Yet we do so, for we are bound to see that his horizon was extremely limited. He had never travelled, except to France (and Mary was taken ill in the usual way before they returned), he had never seen the glories of Rome, the beauty of Florence and Venice; he had never been to India or to Russia, nor to America or Greece. And is it not significant that all his dreams were of cities abroad? Surely he longed sometimes to enlarge his sphere! And had he done so, would not his work have grown in interest and variety? What letters he would have written!

Yet we must be grateful for those already in our possession, that unique collection which gives us such an intimate picture of his life. Here we are able to share all his moods. We sit with him and Mary in their tiny drawing-room at Islington, where the walls were hung with his portraits of the poets, and his 'Hogarths'. On the mantelpiece are his dainty china Chelsea shepherds and shepherdesses, which were family relics. We share with him, too, the turkey sent to him by Crabb Robinson every Christmas, the hares and pheasants which came to him from his friend Allsop, those succulent oysters which he and his friends devoured so happily, and the dinner which was given in his honour at the London Tavern. He apparently, on this occasion, attempted to make a speech, but got no further than 'Gentlemen. . . .'

The small characteristics which are inseparable from Lamb come back to us too. We remember how he loathed the very name of winter, how intensely he disliked moving house, and how he would have nothing to do with politics. He referred to the devil as 'that old spider', and red ink as 'clerks' blood'; he loved to walk through the streets of London at night, especially if he was feeling melancholy. (It was a certain cure.) We remember, too, that he very wisely never read criticisms of his own work.

Indeed, Charles Lamb was 'a rare being', and as he extends his hand to us across the years we grasp it with gratitude and affection, like an old friend. He had 'as fine a heart as ever beat in human breast' and his letters and essays are unique in their very special quality.

William Hazlitt

1778–1830

'MANKIND are a herd of knaves and fools. It is necessary to join the crowd or get out of their way in order
not to be trampled to death by them.'
So said William Hazlitt, and not only was it his considered
opinion, but it explains the whole tragedy of his life. Nothing
would induce him to 'join the crowd', and nothing would induce
him either to get out of their way. So although he was not
trampled to death, he was jostled on every side and he suffered
accordingly.

What a lonely, isolated figure he is, always in a minority of
one! His whole world was a world of thought. 'Thought has in
me cancelled pleasure', he said, 'and this dark forehead, bent
upon truth, is the rock on which all affection has split.' Reared in
an atmosphere of metaphysics, philosophy and religion, he inherited from his father very strong views on the rights and
liberties of man, and a positive loathing for servility, tyranny and
vested interests. But he never learned to compromise with the
world. He built up for himself a vast and intricate pinnacle of
thought; it was noble in conception and idealistic in form; only
a thousand years of splendid endeavour could have brought his
vision to perfection, but he refused to abandon it; and when
at last his fine edifice crumbled about him, he became angry and
embittered. Had he been merely a philosopher he might have
made a success of his life, but he was also an artist and a sentimentalist. The past, so full of hopes and dreams, haunted him like
a beautiful ghost, and this frail ghost could never concert with
anything so substantial as reality. The artist in him set the seal of

sorrow upon his life, for his thirst for beauty was never quenched and his passionate desire to create was thwarted. He had wished above all things to be a painter and he had striven frenziedly to realise that ambition. But all to no purpose. In the end he became an essayist and critic, and in this he succeeded admirably, but he never mastered the art of living.

This strange and brooding figure was unusual, even as a child, for we find him at the age of twelve discoursing solemnly, in a letter to his father, on such serious questions as liberty and slavery. Next we see him in adolescence, a difficult and nervous boy. Sometimes he would shut himself up all day long, and then at night he would wander out into the moonlight, alone.

But this picture of the boy is a very shadowy one. When Hazlitt emerges into the full light of day he is a striking yet pathetic figure. He had a 'noble head' set off by rich black curls, but the face was pale, and the eager, restless eyes peered suspiciously from under the overhanging brows. He was painfully shy, and entered a room 'as if he had been brought back to it in custody'. It is clear, in fact, that in an age when it was necessary to hold one's head high, to speak well, to dress finely, to bow handsomely, and to be courteous and affable, Hazlitt cut a very poor figure. That he was a genius was not enough. Society expected far more than that.

There can be no doubt, in fact, that Hazlitt was a genius of a very rare order; he was a born critic, one of the finest and deepest thinkers of the day, and as sincere and honest a man as ever breathed. But he could not see that in the hurly burly of life it is necessary to hide one's wounds, to lick them in secret, to put up a brave front. Had he held his head high and laughed at his enemies the world would have taken him for a fine fellow. Hazlitt was, in fact, a martyr to that all too familiar complaint, an inferiority complex. His attempts to become, like his father, a Unitarian Minister, had not succeeded, so he had decided to become an author. Rousseau was his god, and he wept bitterly over the *Confessions*. It was at this time, too, that he met Coleridge, having walked ten miles into Shrewsbury to hear him preach.

WILLIAM HAZLITT
From the replica by William Bewick of his drawing of 1822

Later, the men spent some weeks together at Nether Stowey, where Hazlitt was also introduced to Wordsworth. Was it the company of these two brilliant men which quenched his ambition? At all events Hazlitt decided to forget literature and become a painter.

We see him next, therefore, living in Bohemian London, a very shy and silent youth but extremely good-looking, with delicately modelled features and fine intelligent eyes, The artist's models in those days were almost all middle-aged prostitutes, and to Hazlitt, reared in an almost Puritan atmosphere, the life led by these art students was a revelation. There can be no doubt that the knowledge he gained of women at this time did him infinite harm. He was not popular, either, as he had a difficult temper and was sometimes offensive in argument. Indeed, how could a man of such outstanding intelligence suffer fools gladly? Every immature opinion irritated him, as he had already soared far above his companions in thought. How could he make allowances for the inferior intellect, the poor judgement, the vulgar uninformed taste? Was it not inevitable that he generally found himself alone? For who wishes to be crushed by a weight of argument which is so far above one's head that it cannot even be grasped?

Hazlitt, however, was almost unaware of his isolation, for in order to master the technique of painting he worked and studied unceasingly, night and day. Rembrandt and Titian were his idols, and he lived in a glorious dream-world of pictures. He declared that a new heaven and new earth stood before him, and after four years he went to France, as part of his training, to copy pictures in the Louvre; he was deliriously happy.

On his return to England he began, with great enthusiasm, to paint portraits, but his portraits of Coleridge and Wordsworth were severely criticised, and he was hurt and humiliated. Southey declared that Coleridge looked like 'a horse-stealer on his trial', and Wordsworth, according to another critic, reminded one of a man on the gallows 'deeply affected by a fate he felt to be deserved'.

Finally Hazlitt painted a portrait of a handsome young man, which was a failure. It was an experience common to most young artists, but Hazlitt, sensitive to an almost morbid degree, was convinced that he had chosen the wrong vocation, that he had no real talent. He lost all confidence in himself, threw down his brushes and decided to paint no more. It was a terrible grief to him, a grief such as only an artist can understand, for Art was his life, his love, the very reason for his existence. And now he was left desolate; life seemed to stretch before him like an arid desert, barren, bare, sunless, the trees withered, the birds silent; his misery could not be put into words, and he cared not whether he lived or died. Yet life, it seemed, must go on; and so it was that he began to write.

Hazlitt became an author because there was nothing else to which he could turn, and although at first he found composition extremely difficult, at least he had plenty to say. His mind was on fire with ideas of every kind and on every subject. Most of his early work was dreary hack work, but now at least he was free to speak his mind as a champion of democracy, a valiant upholder of the poor and downtrodden, and an unashamed admirer of Napoleon. Napoleon was the chief enemy of England at that time, but Hazlitt had watched his career 'like a lover'. He had watched him, with great glee, bring the royal houses of France to their knees, and whatever Napoleon did Hazlitt justified.

Yet there were other matters, too, on which he felt strongly, for in England at that time trade was bad, prices were high, many of the poor were starving, and thousands were in great distress. Hazlitt could not remain silent while the poor suffered. He therefore attacked the Government's policy right and left. But few agreed with him, for was not the war responsible for this misery? And was not war a necessary evil?

It was at this time, in fact, that Hazlitt made so many enemies, and henceforth he was a target for every venomous shaft shot from the bows of his adversaries. Among them *Blackwood's Magazine*, was his bitterest critic—*Blackwood's* whose criticism had crushed Keats and half-maddened Shelley. The first twenty-five volumes of *Blackwood's Magazine* made incessant scurrilous and furious attacks upon the person, private character, motives, talents and moral and religious principles of Hazlitt. 'Ass, blockhead, fool, idiot, quack, villain, infidel' are merely a few of the epithets, applied to him. And Hazlitt was so vulnerable that he returned blow for blow, thus giving a great advantage to his opponents.

Poor Hazlitt! He was no rich dilettante, writing from the depths of a luxurious arm-chair, but he was entirely dependent on his writings for his daily bread. Literary work was atrociously paid in any case, and these criticisms lowered the opinion of his capacity with booksellers, and so drained away his livelihood.

Had Hazlitt been a happy man he would not, perhaps, have married, as he was obviously unsuited to domestic life. Yet marry he did, for women were necessary to him, and secretly he longed to be loved and appreciated. He was, in fact, capable of intense devotion, but Sarah Stoddart, who became Mrs Hazlitt, was quite unsuitable. He soon saw that she 'despised him and his abilities'. Apparently she was a florid, hoydenish, mercenary woman, undomesticated, untidy, unromantic and selfish. The decencies and comforts of life meant nothing to her. Why should she be bothered to rise early, or light a fire, or put curtains at the windows? Nor, apparently, could she be bothered with children, for when her first little boy died, before he had reached his second year, the post mortem revealed that he had swallowed a bag of white paint, a small hearth brush, two golden pippins and a letter from Mary Lamb! Hazlitt was grieved beyond words at the loss of this dearly loved child, whom he had always treated with great tenderness. Nor apparently did matters mend when the couple moved to London, for Haydon gives us a depressing picture of Hazlitt's way of life at this time.

Haydon had been invited to the christening of Hazlitt's second child, but when he arrived there was no one to greet him except Mrs Hazlitt, who sat by the fire 'quite dejected' and still in a bed-gown. Hazlitt, however, returned shortly with the astonishing news that he had forgotten to order the parson, so had been vainly searching for one. In the meantime the guests began to arrive, but there was still no sign of a meal. At last, however, a maid laid the cloth, put down knives and forks in a heap, and brought in a dish of 'cold, yellow, waxy' potatoes and a great piece of beef 'with a bone like a battering ram.' Of wine there was none, and Haydon returned home thoroughly disconsolate, having decided that even the company of Hazlitt and Lamb could not reconcile him 'to such violation of all the decencies of life'.

In this tall narrow house in Westminster Milton had once lived, so Hazlitt had placed an engraved stone on the wall: *To Milton Prince of Poets*. Yet Hazlitt's only contribtion to the interior decorations was to scribble notes of essays on the walls right up to the ceiling. Was this, we wonder, to save the expense of paper? Certainly he was continually in debt.

So here we see Hazlitt again, far more careworn, very much greyer about the temples, and sadly in need of money. Debts, debts, debts! How they haunted him! And whether he was writing an essay, or an article for a paper, or a treatise on philosophy, he was always working against the clock. It was misery! It was torture! And constantly lurking in the shadows were his enemies. Whatever he wrote now was suspect, for they would not let him alone, and the irritation and indignation they caused bowed him down. How could he, with a knife in his heart, greet his friends with affability and a genial smile? Sometimes he was invited to the houses of rich men to dine, but he felt uneasy, uncertain of himself. He was terrified of servants, and of those suave, unruffled, well-groomed men who could always command their tempers, who could even discuss his hero Napoleon with a well-bred smile! No one knew how he suffered on these occasions; no one would believe how humiliated and miserable he was. And yet he realised, without conceit, that he had a far finer mind than any of these men. He could see through them so clearly. He could have demolished them in argument in five minutes. But the graces! The graces! He did not possess the graces.

Money, too, was needed in order to uphold one's dignity, for how could a shabby man take his place in society? One was set down as a failure at first glance. The idea, therefore, was suggested to him that he should give lectures on Philosophy, much in the style of the essays he had written, some of which had been greatly admired by his friends. It is true that he had no experience of lecturing and that he was intensely nervous. But what others could do he could do. And to keep the wolf from the door was an urgent necessity.

Hazlitt's first lecture was delivered in the winter of 1812 to an audience which consisted chiefly of dissenters (who agreed with him in his hatred of Lord Castlereagh), Quakers (who shared his views on slavery and capital punishment), a few earnest souls thirsting for knowledge, certain of his enemies 'who came to sneer', and a few friends who genuinely admired him. He arrived with a lecture which was calculated to last three hours, but was told on arrival that he was only to be allowed one hour. This awful news threw him into a panic, as the lecture was so closely reasoned that he could not possibly shorten it at the last moment, nor was he capable of putting it on one side and speaking merely from notes. He therefore read the whole thing through at a tremendous pace, standing with downcast eyes which never for a moment rested on his audience. The effect, of course, was nothing less than stupefying.

Amongst the audience was his brother-in-law, Dr. Stoddart, whose caustic comment was, 'This will never do.' Other friends expressed their sympathy with the unfortunate lecturer, and Hazlitt went through agonies of shame. But he was in debt, money must be earned, and the lectures had been advertised as a course; therefore, they must go on. It is to his great credit, therefore, that he gave eight lectures and that they were successful, for in time he improved and learnt to adjust himself to his audience.

It would seem at this time, indeed, that Hazlitt was about to live, to taste like other men the joy in the fruition of his labours, the pleasures of friendship, the happiness of family life. He had, in fact, his moments; there were times when he could escape into the country for a while and revel in pastoral pleasures:

Is not this wild rose sweet without a comment? Does not this daisy leap to my heart, set in its coat of emerald. . . . How fine it is to enter some old town, walled and turreted, just at the approach of nightfall, or to come to some straggling village, with the lights streaming through the surrounding gloom. . . .

And sometimes Beauty blazed forth in all her finery:

I look out of my window and see that the shower has just fallen; the fields look green after it, and a rosy cloud hangs over the brow of the hill; a lily expands its petals in the moisture, dressed in its lovely green and white; a shepherd has just brought some pieces of turf with daisies and grass for his young mistress to make a bed for her skylark. . . .

On days like this the difficulties and humiliations of life were forgotten. Sometimes he would tramp for miles, with the heavenly sky above his head, and the grass beneath his feet; every vista brought a new delight. But alas, how fleeting is beauty! The sky, the green fields and the rosy cloud can be blotted out so quickly; the dark clouds gather, and the storm burst upon the landscape. . . . So it was with Hazlitt. When the news arrived that his idol, Napoleon, had abdicated, Hazlitt was utterly shattered; to him it was nothing short of a calamity. He felt that the blood of almost six million men had been shed in vain. His hopes were raised again, however, when Napoleon reappeared on the coast and marched triumphantly to Paris. But the victory of Waterloo followed, and Hazlitt's desolation was complete. He was pro-strated in mind and body, and except to those who saw him his misery was unbelievable. He wandered about the streets of London for weeks, unwashed, unshaven, 'hardly sober by day and always intoxicated by night. He had hoped in his lifetime to see—as he said—'some prospect of good to mankind' such as that with which his life had begun. But what hope could there be now? To him Waterloo was not a triumph of liberty, but a triumph of autocracy. And when finally the Emperor was im-prisoned on St Helena Hazlitt was roused to a passionate anger; he could not even discuss the subject without becoming abusive.

So while his countrymen were rejoicing in a great national victory and the final crushing of the enemy Hazlitt walked alone, friendless, shunned, forgotten. Well might he say, at the end, 'My soul has indeed remained in its original bondage, dark, obscure, with longings infinite and unsatisfied; my heart, shut up in the prison-house of this rude clay, has never found, nor will it ever find, a heart to speak to.'

But if his views alienated him from most of his friends, he deliberately lashed out and cut himself off from the poets, Southey, Wordsworth and Coleridge, for they in the past had agreed with his views; they had been even more revolutionary in speech, yet now they had ranged themselves on the side of power; they were quite complacent about the turn events had taken. Traitors, traitors, all of them! And at the first opportunity Hazlitt attacked them with biting sarcasm. It was unwise, for Wordsworth was quick to retaliate and began to circulate an unpleasant story of Hazlitt's flight from the Lake district, and suggested that such a man was not fit for decent society. No one could disprove the story, but Hazlitt's enemies, of course, were delighted to enlarge upon the incident, and even his friends eyed him with distaste. *Blackwood's Magazine* also attacked and slandered him again, although when he instituted proceedings they paid damages and costs; but the harm was done.

Yet life had to go on, and he had learnt at least one lesson; he had stopped drinking, and never again did he touch alcohol. It was at this time that he gave another very successful course of lectures, on English poetry. This work, however, was a great strain on his health and temper, and at the end of 1819 his domestic affairs came to grief, his home in Westminster was broken up, and his wife and child returned to the country. He went into rooms, lonely, embittered and sad. And then, although he was forty-two, he fell in love.

The object of Hazlitt's affections was his landlady's daughter, another Sarah, and this was love at first sight, the strangest, most passionate love. The girl was about twenty, pale, dark, demure and gentle. Hazlitt thought her very beautiful. He gave her presents of fine books exquisitely bound in red velvet, and begged her to promise to marry him if he could divorce his wife. She would promise nothing, however. But he was not deterred, and he interpreted her shyness and strange silences as evidence of a rare chastity. This was love indeed, and if she could not be his then he was utterly lost. Did he ever pause to ask himself what he had to offer—this brilliant, embittered and difficult man? Did he ever pause to wonder how he could possibly make her happy? She was simple, uneducated and unintelligent. It is unlikely that she could ever have understood him or sympathised with his dark moods.

Finally he went to Scotland to get a divorce, and with the collusion of his wife he produced the necessary evidence, but when he returned to London some weeks later, a free man and full of hope, Sarah received him coldly and confessed that she already had a lover.

The shock drove him almost demented; he could neither eat nor sleep, and in his agony he told his story to everyone, even to strangers. 'She was my life; I have lost her, myself, heaven, and am doomed to hell.' This was the tone of his lament, and to ease his mind he wrote an account of the whole affair (*Liber Amoris*) and published it, anonymously. But the identity of the author became known—it was inevitable—and the results were extremely painful.

Yet it would seem that Hazlitt did not despair of happiness, for in 1824, to the surprise of his friends, he married again, the widow of a barrister. She was a well-bred, gracious woman with private means, and she made his new home at 10, Down Street, Piccdilly, a very pleasant one. Eventually they travelled together in France, Italy and Switzerland. But by the autumn of 1827 the second Mrs Hazlitt had left him and he was alone in London again. He had taken a small back room at 6, Frith Street, Soho. But he was no longer handsome; the dark curls had turned grey and his face had become 'hard, weather-beaten and saturnine'. Certainly the passionate eyes threw out their challenge as fiercely as ever, but there was a look of suffering about him that repelled. His health was bad, too, so that writing—for one must write in order to live—had become a burden. There were compensations, of course, for his grown-up son had become a great joy to him, and Hazlitt had written a life of Napoleon, a book on which he set great hopes.

Yet ill-fortune still dogged him, as the publisher of his first two volumes of Napoleon went bankrupt, which meant a sad loss of income, and the work attracted little notice or praise. He is said, a little before his death, to have met Horne, and said to him: 'I have carried a volcano in my breast for the last three hours up and down Pall Mall; I have striven mortally to quench, to quell it, but it will not. Can you lend me a shilling? I have not tasted food for two days.'

Hazlitt died when he was fifty-two years of age, but his health had long been deteriorating. He had written 'I should like to have some friendly hand to consign me to the grave', and his wish was granted, for a few friends were at his bedside when he drew his last breath. He was buried in the churchyard of St Ann's, Soho, and Charles Lamb, faithful to the last, attended his funeral.

It is impossible to read Hazlitt's Essays without admiration, for they are so eloquent, earnest and original; they are so rich in knowledge and wisdom, and so finely and strongly expressed. His criticism is glowingly acute, gorgeously clear. But his work is particularly interesting because it reveals the most striking characteristic of the man himself. His essays are fair and reasonable, but suddenly, in order to illustrate his point, he draws on his personal experiences; he has suffered and he cannot be silent about it. Then when the passion has subsided the theme of the essays is resumed and he is calm and wise again. These passages, of course, mar the intellectual detachment of the essay, yet how much closer they draw us to the author himself; their very poignancy makes him stand out with a dramatic vividness. There he is, the intense individualist, the fiery advocate of liberty and justice, the lonely sentimentalist, filled with nostalgia for the past, aching for the pure love of women, but embittered by his many failures.

That Hazlitt knew of this fault—if fault it is—is almost certain, but the temptation to give way to it is too strong for him. He could not, as did Montaigne and Lamb, reveal his personality by intimate, light, personal touches; he had no gift for such writing, but only by these sudden bursts of passionate feeling, always personal, invariably bitter.

So although Hazlitt never becomes endeared to us—for compassion is the only feeling he rouses—yet we close the book with a deep sigh, for there are so many pictures of him we should like to contemplate a little longer. We see him as a schoolboy, shyly presenting his young partner with a large bunch of lilac after a country dance; we see him sitting by his cottage fire, writing, while the partridge waits for him in the oven; we see him gazing thoughtfully at the tombs of the Knights Templar in the old Temple Church. And last of all we hear him weeping in the night (he wept easily) because he had been dreaming again of the pictures he had copied in Paris, seventeen years before.

We remember, too, all sorts of odd things about him—that he addressed everyone as 'Sir', even children, that his room was hung with prints of Claude Lorraine, that he loved conversation —his own conversation could be delightful—and that he thought it worth while to climb four flights of stairs in order to talk with Charles Lamb. We remember with admiration, too, that he 'never wrote a line that licked the dust', that he has left us a capital portrait of Charles Lamb, and that that delightful man thought him 'one of the finest and wisest spirits breathing'.

If Hazlitt failed in his friendships and came to grief in his love affairs it was because he never learnt to 'skate gracefully over the surface of life'. He was always falling through the ice, floundering in the depths and coming up against the most painful obstacles.

But such courage, integrity and nobility of purpose are rare, and this fine essayist and brilliant critic should be honoured accordingly.

James Henry Leigh Hunt

1784–1859

ON a certain afternoon in the year 1834 Carlyle paid a call at a house in Chelsea, a call which obviously left a vivid impression on his mind, for he has taken the trouble to record it. The house was one which suggested both elegance and order within, but to his surprise he was met on entering by 'four or five beautiful, strange, gypsy-looking children running about in undress', and all was 'hugger-mugger'. The rooms were untidy and dusty, the carpets were ragged, and the mistress of the house —who should, of course have received him—lay asleep on cushions.

'An indescribable dream-like household!' thought Carlyle. But such was the home of James Henry Leigh Hunt, poet, editor, essayist and critic. And upstairs in his study Carlyle found the man himself, a tall, graceful figure and undoubtedly handsome, with his raven black hair, beautifully shaped head, fine dark eyes and clear brown complexion. He was wearing 'a loose-flowing cloud of a printed nightgown', a costume he invariably wore when he was writing.

But did this elegant gentleman apologise for his dress, or his slovenly wife, or his strange children, or the shabbiness and disorder of his house? Not at all. Perfectly self-possessed, he received Carlyle like a king; and soon they were talking—of philosophy, and the prospects of man, of heaven and hell, of Dante and Petrarch. Leigh Hunt was an excellent conversationalist, and it was not for nothing that Mrs Carlyle christened him—later on— 'The talking nightingale'. Indeed, Emerson and De Quincey both declared that Leigh Hunt had the finest manners of any literary man they had ever met.

Here then is a glimpse of a writer who filled his niche with unusual grace and brilliance. All his life he battled against 'a sea of troubles'—debts, ill-health, a large family, imprisonment and poverty—but he remained to the end charming, unembittered, enthusiastic and honourable.

Leigh Hunt was the son of a lawyer, who later became a parson, but who originally hailed from Barbados. He 'had a knack of publishing ironical tracts for the times'—a knack his son certainly inherited—and it is said that his eloquence as a preacher attracted large and fashionable congregations. But in spite of his apparent success he too saw the inside of a prison. Leigh Hunt's mother was a tall, dark, handsome lady who once took off her flannel petticoat—in a gateway—to give to a destitute woman. To her Leigh Hunt owed his love of literature and flowers, and his warm sympathy for all unfortunates.

Leigh Hunt was educated within the monastic walls of Christ's Hospital, but his schooldays were spent in the luxurious house of Benjamin West, 'historical painter to His Majesty', a house of large pictures and many statues; and from the old Academician in his white woollen gown the future author learnt something of painting. But Leigh Hunt's passion for literature soon showed itself, and at twenty he was already a dramatic critic whose work was attracting notice. He was determined 'to change the thought of England' and he began to write with passionate enthusiasm on all the burning questions of the day. Anything in the nature of social injustice roused him to fierce indignation. He possessed, also, a mischievous itch to ridicule and expose all that was false or pretentious, and the whip of his satire lashed out unmercifully. It was not that he was vindictive by nature; he was merely impatient of hypocrisy and humbug; and as for great names, they did not in the least deter him; they rather spurred him on. So he was soon in trouble, and was finally prosecuted for his views on military flogging. He was acquitted but not silenced, and satirical articles continued to pour from his pen.

JAMES HENRY LEIGH HUNT
From the painting by Samuel Lawrence, 1837

Those were the days when personal hostility was carried to excessive lengths in periodicals; nothing was sacred or safe from misrepresentation—personal habits, appearances, connections, domestic affairs, etc. Leigh Hunt was therefore merely following the literary fashion, but he continually overstepped the mark, and as a result he made many enemies. Magazines were started, and although they rarely lasted very long, yet each one put forward some new theory for human progress. Indeed, he soon made a reputation as a forceful and fearless opponent in controversy. And how he worked! Creditors might thunder at the door, demanding to be paid, but he remained unperturbed. A friend could always be found to come to the rescue with a loan; indeed, he had the most wonderful friends.

But somehow he never succeeded in straightening out his financial affairs. Was it because he did not know his multiplication tables (he admitted this sad fact) or because he was by nature utterly improvident and unpractical? Perhaps Shelley could have told us, for the two were intimate friends. It was Shelley who generously insisted on paying Leigh Hunt's debts—once to the extent of £1,400—and also lent him large sums of money.

Yet if Leigh Hunt got into debt, he was himself unfailingly generous to others. He and his friends, in fact, were all in debt to each other. Peter borrowed to pay Paul, and Paul borrowed to pay back Peter; the lending and borrowings went back and forth like a shuttle. Children were born, and of course had to be clothed and fed, so one borrowed wildly. But soon one's dear friend arrived with a pitiful tale; he was in imminent danger of going to a debtors' prison, his wife was ailing, and the bailiffs had distrained on the furniture. There was no food in the house, and the children sat on the bare floor, weeping and wailing, by the light of a farthing candle. One's heart bled for them; the tears ran down one's cheeks in sympathy . . . and out came the generous purse, and fifty pounds or so would be paid out smilingly, ungrudgingly. 'Take it, my dear fellow, take it. You are more than welcome.' It was a fantastic state of affairs, and one barely knew who was in prison for debt and who was just coming out. But somehow life went on.

Haydon, the painter, always impecunious, always in a muddle, declared that Leigh Hunt behaved 'nobly' to him. He offered him 'always a plate at his table' until his large picture was finished. And later, again, the Hunts 'nobly assisted him at the cost of great personal deprivation'. As for Leigh Hunt himself, Haydon thought him 'as fine a specimen of a London editor as could be imagined, assuming yet moderate, sarcastic yet genial . . . He had an open affectionate manner which was most engaging.'

It must not be supposed, however, that this delightful man was all grace, charm and wit, for he was also a man of fearless moral courage, and he was willing at any time to sacrifice his own interests for the sake of fair play, liberty and the rights of the individual. Hypocrisy and cruel abuses must be exposed, and as the editor of *The Examiner* he was well able to set out his views. Nor did he attempt to mince his words. But at last—it was inevitable—he went too far, for he rashly published an article which ridiculed the Prince Regent. What he said of that debauched and unworthy Prince was only too true, but it was bitterly and contemptuously expressed, and Leigh Hunt had to pay the penalty. He was sentenced to two years' imprisonment and a fine of £500. It was a savage punishment for such an offence, and Shelley at once made 'a princely offer' to pay the fine. But Leigh Hunt felt that he could not accept.

We see Leigh Hunt, therefore, as witty and amusing as ever, in Horsemonger Lane Gaol, where finally his wife and child were allowed to join him. Another little Leigh Hunt was on the way, and was, indeed, born in prison. Yet how courageously Leigh Hunt had taken his punishment! He had turned the prison rooms into a home by papering the walls with a trellis of roses, and the ceiling with clouds and sky. Then he had set up his bookcases and busts, and installed a piano. There was 'probably not a handsomer room on that side of the water', he declared. 'It must have come out of a fairy tale', said Charles Lamb. As for the dingy prison yard, Leigh Hunt turned it into a pleasant garden by planting flowering shrubs; scarlet runners were also trained to grow up the trellises, and flowers were induced to flourish in the borders. There was no dearth of visitors, either, for Charles and Mary Lamb came (laden with baskets of fruit) and Hazlitt, Byron, Tom Moore, Haydon and Sir John Swinburne. Jeremy Bentham, the white-haired philosopher, also arrived, and in spite of his sixty-five years, played battledore and shuttlecock with his friend in the prison yard.

Leigh Hunt suffered, of course, in many ways, for his health was bad—the gaoler gloomily insisted that he would never live to go out—and it was depressing to hear the prisoners in the cells below dragging their chains. Nevertheless, he continued to write, and his notebooks were filled with poetry. He grew, in fact, almost attached to the place, for when he found himself a free man at last—a great moment, surely!—suddenly the whole business of life appeared to be 'a hideous impertinence' and he was bewildered and unhappy.

But how, we wonder, did Mrs Leigh Hunt take these misfortunes? Apparently with patient resignation, for she never complained, although her health was extremely delicate and she vomited blood on the least provocation. On the other hand, she was hardly an asset to her talented husband, for although she could read verses very finely she was a bad housekeeper and the greatest borrower in London. She borrowed consistently and continually—a few tumblers, teacups or teaspoons, a little tea or porridge, a brass fender or a pair of irons. Mrs Carlyle was never surprised to see one of the beautiful 'gypsy-looking children' on her doorstep asking prettily for the loan of these things. But unfortunately the borrowed articles were rarely returned intact. One teaspoon or tumbler was sure to be missing, and Mrs Carlyle, who was Scotch and took the greatest pride in her household possessions, found it difficult to hide her displeasure.

It was in 1821 that Leigh Hunt's greatest piece of folly took shape, for at the suggestion of Shelley—who lent him £150 towards the venture—he decided to take his entire family to Italy. He had six young children at the time, but his plan was to secure new aid to his prospects and 'new friends to the cause of liberty'. 'Put your music and your books on board a vessel and you will have no more trouble', said Shelley. Alas, for the poets of this world! Shelley, wrapped in shining visions, was hardly capable of giving sound advice on such a matter. The time was autumn and the weather was cold and blustery. To board a vessel was easy, even accompanied by fifty-six volumes of the *Parnaso Italiano*, but to be forced to occupy one small cabin with a wife and six small children when a terrific storm was raging was a nightmare. The children were placed in the bunks, and Leigh Hunt and his wife lay on the floor, but the ship, which incidentally carried a cargo of fifty barrels of gunpowder, could not make headway in such weather, and after tossing on the heaving ocean for some days returned to Ramsgate. About a month later they set off again, only to encounter even more tempestuous storms; sails were carried away, lightning and thunder terrified the children, and according to Leigh Hunt fifteen hundred sail were wrecked on the coast of Jutland alone. So again the voyage was postponed, and the ship returned to Plymouth.

Five months later, however, the whole family embarked once more, and finally arrived in Italy, where for a time they occupied the ground floor of Byron's 'salmon coloured' mansion in Pisa. Byron was writing *Don Juan*, under the influence of gin and water, and sang continually. He wore a cap of velvet, a loose nankin jacket with white trousers, and 'his hair in thin ringlets about his throat.' His flaxen-haired mistress completed the household. But it must be admitted that he and Leigh Hunt (whom Byron addressed as 'Leontius' (an idea of Shelley's) did not see eye to eye for long, and relations soon became strained. Perhaps Mrs Leigh Hunt also had something to do with the matter; perhaps she borrowed too ruthlessly. Certainly Byron disliked her, and was rude and peevish.

But more serious troubles were to come, for soon Leigh Hunt's money came to an end, and his wife was declared to be 'in a decline', the doctor stating that she would scarcely last a year. Then came the awful tragedy of Shelley; he was drowned and his body was cast up on to the shore. Shelley, the flower of genius! He had been a wonderful friend to Leigh Hunt, but never again would he sit talking round the lamp, or sail paper boats on the pond at Hampstead. The shrill voice was silenced, the fair complexion marred, the brown hair tangled with wet seaweed. And now that he was dead Mrs Leigh Hunt remembered all sorts of odd things about him—how he adored flowers, and loved watching the fireflies, how he would sit poring over Plato, or Homer, or the Bible, that he had a queer habit of drawing elm and ash trees on the walls or on his manuscripts. At Eton they had called him 'mad Shelley' and had pelted him with mud, but he had had the kindest, most generous heart, and he had loved Leigh Hunt. . . .

Then remembering Shelley reminded her, too, of poor Keats. He had stayed with them for a time at Hampstead, but the street cries and ballad singers from the terrace had bothered him dreadfully, and he had not been able to work well. She had much admired his beautiful poem 'La belle dame sans merci' which had appeared in Leigh Hunt's magazine, *The Indicator*. He too had been cut off in the flower of his youth. As for Byron, that odd creature, he had gone to Greece. He, she remembered, had liked riding on the children's large rocking-horse . . . Such a difficult man!

Leigh Hunt and his family returned to England in 1825 and he then proceeded to write a book of recollections, chiefly concerning Byron and his contemporaries. The book was written hurriedly, for Leigh Hunt, as usual, was financially embarrassed. But it was impossible to reveal the details of his friendship with Byron without toppling the poet from his pedestal, and the public were horrified at this criticism of their romantic hero. For them—for they knew nothing of Byron's private life—the author of *Childe Harold* was something between a god and a saint. Therefore they turned bitterly on Leigh Hunt for destroying their illusions. He, in a fine frenzy to justify himself, made the mistake of answering those criticisms. It was, however, Byron who eventually won the day.

This book, in fact, caused Leigh Hunt much unhappiness. Yet

he was never depressed for long, and by the year 1840 he had written a play, *A Legend of Florence*, which was produced at Covent Garden Theatre. It was well received and ran for fifteen or twenty nights, the two benefit performances alone producing four hundred guineas for the author, a sum which should have cleared his debts. But it did nothing of the sort, so finally Mary Shelley gave him an allowance of £120 a year, and in 1847 he was also granted a civil pension of £200 a year, allowances which did much to ease the burden of his old age.

Some of the last years of Leigh Hunt's life were spent at 32, Edwardes Square, Kensington, and here he wrote his memoirs and many other books. He was now 'a beautiful old man' and wore a handsome velvet coat 'with a vandyck collar of lace about a foot deep'. His manners, too, were as fine as ever, and he still took intense delight in all that was beautiful. A blossoming tree or a sparkling frost would send him into ecstacies, and the bowl of flowers on his grand piano, at which he loved to sing and play, was always a feature of his room. He had a passion for Haydn, Mozart and Purcell. 'This is a beautiful world, Mr Patmore', he said, on greeting the poet, for visitors came now as on a pilgrimage—the philosopher Emerson, and Nathaniel Hawthorn and Dickens. He was delighted to see them, for he had few contemporaries. Lamb, Hazlitt, Haydon, Shelley, Keats, Byron, Wordsworth, Tom Moore and Southey were all dead; he had outlived them all.

But was the house, we wonder, still 'hugger-mugger', as Carlyle called it? There is no record, for, alas, Carlyle no longer came. All we know is that the 'beautiful gypsy-looking children' had grown up—two had died—and Mrs Leigh Hunt was almost crippled with rheumatism. She, poor thing, before this illness had seized her, had tried her hand at sculpture, and indeed might have been highly successful, but the worms 'which a modeller cannot avoid in manipulating the fresh clay sickened her so with her crushing them' that she was obliged to abandon this art. She died at the age of sixty-nine, but Leigh Hunt lived on until he was seventy-four.

If we try to estimate Leigh Hunt's place in literature we must admit that he filled it remarkably well. He lived in an age when men of genius were numerous; all his contemporaries were brilliant. Yet he held his own. His essays were written merely for the periodicals of the day; they were not intended for posterity, and he himself would have been surprised that they have lived so long. But surely they will still be read a hundred years hence, for they are inimitable and unique. Has any writer ever described a hot day or a stormy night in London so admirably?—

Now labourers look well resting in their white shirts at the doors of rural ale-houses. Now an elm is fine there, with a seat under it; and horses drink out of the trough, stretching their yearning necks with loosened collars; and the traveller calls for his glass of ale, having been without one for more than ten minutes . . . and now Miss Betsy Wilson, the host's daughter, comes streaming forth in a flowerd gown and earrings, carrying with four of her beautiful fingers the foaming glass. . . . Now cattle stand in water. . . . Now a green lane . . . thick set with hedgerow elms, and having the noise of a brook 'rumbling in pebble stones' is one of the pleasant-est things in the world.

What a wonderful essay this is! And has any other writer put into words just what we feel about 'getting up on cold mornings' and 'the deaths of little children'? It is impossible not to be grate-ful for these essays. As to his poetry, although we should not care to bask perpetually in his gardens with their lilies, bowers of roses, leafy glades and summer-houses, yet this verse has a clean fragrance, a freshness, a greenness, that is all its own. It does not attempt to be the poetry of thought and passion, but it is never-theless wholly delightful. In the right mood it is as refreshing as an April shower.

Yet quite apart from his work Leigh Hunt himself is surely a fine example of sincerity and moral courage. Throughout his life he endeavoured to maintain a standard of truth and justice, and his high principles were utterly incorruptible. He was determined to set the world to rights, but he had no axe to grind—a rare and noble thing. So in thinking of this delightful man we can only regret that we never met him, that we were not able to share in his gaiety, his clever and witty conversation, to bask in his warm friendship. We would give a great deal to have heard his charming voice, to have met him strolling in the meadows of Chelsea with a book under his arm, and even to have entered that 'hugger-mugger' house. We remember that Lamb said he was 'a matchless fireside companion' and that Haydon thought him 'one of the most delightful beings I ever knew'.

Benjamin Robert Haydon

1786–1846

'BY God, sir, it is a victory!' said Hazlitt, holding out two cold fingers to the painter. And the remark was amply justified, for although the picture in question, a huge canvas called 'Solomon's Judgement', may not be considered a masterpiece to-day it was a great triumph in its time.

As for Benjamin Robert Haydon himself, he too had his moments. His life was a chaotic one and at times he suffered intensely, yet he had such a zest for life that he succeeded in wrenching from it more than most of us can even find there. A man who 'painted like a tiger', 'shouted like a savage', 'wept like an infant' (over books), prayed night and day, read the newspaper until he was faint, and entered the sea at Brighton 'like a bull in a green meadow' was no ordinary man. Besides, was he not a friend of Keats, Wordsworth, Shelley, Hazlitt, Leigh Hunt, Charles Lamb, Mary Russell Mitford and Mrs Browning? They all admired him, and some of them wrote sonnets in praise of his work. Miss Mitford declared that such a genius should have been born amongst the Angelos and Raphaels, and Leigh Hunt insisted that he was fit to be numbered in succession to Michael Angelo.

Haydon died a broken-hearted man, and as an artist it is unlikely that he will ever wear the crown of immortality, yet there are two things for which he will always be remembered—a remarkably vivid and interesting autobiography, and an example of a life lived for an ideal. For his ideal in art he sacrificed health, money, comfort and his own good name. In order to paint he felt it worth while to get into debt, to borrow continually from his friends, to implore assistance from great men, to beg shamelessly

147

for credit from shopkeepers, and finally to go to prison. There is no doubt that he was passionately sincere, and if he was misguided he certainly paid for his errors.

It would seem, indeed, that even the day on which Haydon was born was unpropitious, as his father, a Plymouth bookseller, made a note at the time that the weather was 'very dirty' and the wind was W.S.W. Whether his father considered the wind from this direction to be an ill wind or not, no one can say, but certainly the poor man got little pleasure from his son, and he must often have suspected that the elements prevailing at his birth were responsible. It would seem, however, that Haydon's fiery obstinacy owed something to heredity, for the artist declared proudly (later) that his father would have been glad to burn at the stake for his principles.

One cannot escape the conviction that Haydon was doomed to failure in life from the very moment he was placed in his mother's arms, for was ever any man so devoid of the ordinary qualities which smooth one's path in life? He had no tact, no sense of responsibility and no common sense. He could not, apparently, mix with his fellow-men without coming to grief, and in his day, when even a genius could not succeed without patrons, these faults were serious. He quarrelled consistently with patrons and artists, and when others could not see his point of view he was convinced that they were merely conspiring against him. Yet he was far more generously treated than most artists. His friends continually assisted him from their scanty earnings, his landlord allowed him to live rent free for years, picture framers were generous, wine merchants gave him presents, and patrons assisted him over and over again to the extent of hundreds of pounds. As we read his memoirs, in fact, we realise that almost all his troubles were the result of his own folly, and as we see him sink deeper and deeper into the mire we wish only to take him firmly by the shoulders and shake him vigorously. But it is too late.

And yet that strange, misguided man has painted for us an unforgettable portrait. He who consistently refused to paint portraits as a means of livelihood has triumphantly painted his

BENJAMIN ROBERT HAYDON
From the painting by Georgiana Margaretta Zornlin, 1828

own, and whether he is moving with studied composure in aristocratic circles, or standing by the light of a candle in front of one of his huge pictures, he comes vividly before us.

But we see him first as a small boy, difficult, obstinate and determined to be an artist. He is carefully drawing one of his schoolfellows, and his father comes up to him and says 'What are you about, sir? You are putting the eyes in the forehead.' Unfortunately this did not discourage him. He was a boy, too, who liked asking questions, so when one day he came upon his mother weeping bitterly upon the sofa he enquired the reason. 'They have cut off the Queen of France's head,' she sobbed. And so it was. She did not know the Queen of France, and there was absolutely nothing she could do about the tragedy, yet she was determined to weep her heart out. Did not her son perhaps inherit something of this attitude? When a few years later he said goodbye to a young girl of whom he was enamoured he wept for hours in the coach, until, in fact, he saw another pretty girl. Yet there can be no doubt of his sincerity.

We see him next in London (for he had refused to work for his father) painting enthusiastically in a small room in a lodging-house. He was fiercely ambitious and was convinced that the world would very soon ring with his name. In the meantime, his father had promised to support him and Haydon was determined to be a historical painter. But the well-known artist Northcote, to whom he had been given an introduction, thought very differently. 'Historical painter!' he said scornfully. 'Why, ye'll starve with a bundle of straw under your head.' Other painters gave the same advice. Haydon, however, although he knew nothing of the world of art and nothing of his craft, was merely strengthened in his resolve; he would be a historical painter and nothing else. He was convinced that all the crowned heads in Europe would 'hail an English youth who could paint a heroic picture'.

So the work began, and that Haydon made great efforts cannot be denied. He became a pupil at the Academy, he drew and painted feverishly, and he ran about incessantly making contacts and getting introductions to men of influence in the world of art.

But a young painter in those days could not exist without a patron, and Haydon knew it. He was in ecstacies, therefore, when he was introduced to Sir George Beaumont, who was very interested in pictures and a great connoisseur. Sir George asked Haydon to dine with him, an invitation that held immense possibilities. Surely fame now was merely a matter of time; one foot was on the ladder, and he would soon be climbing the dizzy pinnacle. Merciful heavens, it was a prospect which almost overwhelmed him! He had always known that he was born to greatness, and here was the evidence.

But . . . there were snags, for this dining in high society was very alarming to a youth who had never dined with anyone higher than a country parson. Might he not make some frightful *faux pas* which would crush the bright flower of his genius and wither all his hopes? The very thought of Sir George Beaumont's fine house and footmen, etc. terrified him. 'God only knows how I shall go into the room' he thought. He knew nothing of the ways of society. His only asset, in fact, was his audacity, of which he possessed more than his fair share!

We see Haydon, therefore, on the evening of his first dinner-party, nervous, apprehensive, and yet determined to acquit himself well. He shaved until his face was half-skinned, dressed and re-dressed until his back ached, and spent hours before the mirror bowing and talking to himself. At last, 'in a cold perspiration', he drove away. Yet he apparently made a favourable impression at this gathering, for he decided that he was launched into society: he had merely to paint his pictures and the world would be at his feet.

His painting efforts, however, proved to be all too spasmodic, as sometimes he 'idled all day', and he frequently frittered away his precious time in talking, arguing, reading, paying innumerable calls and making elaborate but unnecessary studies. There was no constant and steady application, without which even the greatest genius cannot succeed. One day he spent seventeen hours reading *Clarissa*, yet at the same time he was incurring debts, and his picture was crying to be finished. But whether he had worked or not he never forgot his prayers. Night and morning he was humbly on his knees before his picture imploring God to bless his efforts, to keep him in health, to bring him fame and fortune, and to thwart his enemies. If prayers had been the deciding factor he would have been at the very top of the tree.

It is strange, indeed, that he had so soon made enemies, but with his usual lack of tact he had persuaded his fellow students, without consulting the Academicians, to make a presentation to Fuseli, the Keeper of the Academy. Haydon was elected treasurer of the £50 subscribed, a sum which was more than he had ever possessed in his life. He was terrified of being robbed, so he placed the money under his pillow every night, and beside it he laid a French cavalry sabre for protection. The Academicians were furious at the impudence of this very young man, and this was the beginning of a long-standing quarrel. From that moment Haydon came to loathe all Academicians. He wrote against them, criticised them openly, and went out of his way to make himself obnoxious. Was ever man so foolish in his own interests? He quarrelled also with his kind and generous patrons, and from his own words it is clear that they showed far more patience than he deserved. He admitted, indeed, that he was 'proud of a quarrel with a man of rank'; it was good publicity.

We say to ourselves at this stage of his memoirs, in fact, that we have no patience with the man. He is not only a fool, but a fool in his own interest. Yet when we read how he worked over the Elgin marbles our sympathy goes out to him again, for they were stored in a damp, vault-like room, and sometimes as he worked he was almost frozen with cold. He drew them continually for three months, sometimes for fifteen hours at a stretch, and he was obliged to hold a candle and drawing-board with one hand, and to draw with the other. On one occasion, too, a heavy piece of marble fell down and injured his leg, but nothing could quench his enthusiasm. There is something very pathetic about this dogged persistence, although whether it was necessary is another matter.

There is something very touching, too, about his first picture, for he would not trust anyone but himself to carry this rather large canvas to the Academy. Yet only by the grace of God was it saved from destruction, as he tripped up on the wet pavement and almost landed right in the gutter. The picture was hung in the ante-room, Lord Mulgrave paid him 210 guineas for it, and Haydon was the hero of the hour. The Academicians, however, damned the picture with faint praise, and suddenly he found he was no longer the popular favourite. The great ladies and fashionable folk who had come in crowds to his studio deserted him, and even Lord Mulgrave, who had been so kind, seemed to have cooled off. Haydon was furious, and was certain that the Academicians had injured him deliberately. To add to his worries he was at the end of his financial resources and heavily in debt. Paints, brushes and canvasses were all expensive. As for models, they occasionally worked for him without payment, but most of them were as poor as himself.

His lack of common sense also showed itself at this time in making a cast of a handsome young negro. A wall was built round the man, and seven bushels of plaster were poured, in, so that it might set round him at once. The plaster floated the model up to the neck, but the wretched man, hemmed in on all sides with stone, was unable to breathe. Haydon realised just in time what was happening, and by cracking the mould released him, but the man would have been dead in another few seconds.

Yet it cannot be denied that life was good in many ways for Haydon, for he had some excellent friends. There was Charles Lamb, 'quaint and incomprehensible', and Leigh Hunt, 'a delightful man and extremely witty'; There was Hazlitt, an intellectual croaker, but brilliantly clever and good company. Then there was Wordsworth; 'never did any man so beguile the time'; and last but not least there was Keats; Haydon worshipped Keats. What wonderful conversation these men had when they met together! On one or two occasions Shelley also made up the party, and although he and Haydon argued a little—for Shelley's views on atheism could not go unanswered—yet how delightfully the time passed in such company! Debts and dunning tradesmen were forgotten. Though one had pawned one's clothes, watch and books, and owed two years' rent to one's landlord, yet the company of immortal poets and fine authors made up for it.

In the meantime, Haydon's great canvasses grew larger and larger. He was warned that there would be no sale for them, but the man who believed 'that he had something in him of Nelson' was not to be deterred by advice. Hazlitt said to him one day, when he was asked to admire one of his friend's pictures, 'Why did you begin it so large? A smaller canvas might have concealed your faults. You'll never sell it.' And Northcote said 'I'll bet my very life you never do.' They were right, of course, but Haydon retorted that if he had possessed a room four hundred feet long, two hundred feet high and four hundred feet wide he would have ordered a canvas 399.6 feet long by 199.6 feet high.

His enormous picture 'Jerusalem', in fact, took six years to paint, yet it is safe to say that a first-class artist could have painted it in less than a year. However, at great expense Haydon hired a large gallery in which to display this magnificently framed and draped picture, and he sent off eight hundred invitations to the private view, to everyone of note in London. All the foreign Ambassadors in London were invited, and the nobility, all the Bishops, all the great beauties, all the highest military officers, and the Ministers and their ladies. Mrs Siddons, too, was invited, and in 'deep, loud, tragic tones' she solemnly pronounced her opinion; she approved of the picture; and that, of course, decided the matter. The poet Rogers, however, made a very significant remark: 'Mr Haydon', he said, 'your ass is the saviour of your picture.'

From this exhibition Haydon made a clear profit of £1,298. He also exhibited the picture in Glasgow and Edinburgh, making a profit of £3,000. How unkind, therefore, he thought his creditors to press for payment! Indeed, after satisfying the most obnoxious he was left with rather less money than he had expected. What a scandal it was, too, that a man of genius should not be entirely supported by the state! He considered that he should be commissioned to paint altar pieces for churches and cathedrals. He did not realise, apparently, that English churches, owing to the climate, are generally damp and cold, and that oil paintings, therefore, would soon deteriorate. Indeed, where High Art was concerned Haydon refused to be practical. The truth was he believed that the Academicians were in league against him; they were a set of evil men who wished to destroy him; they were jealous of his powers. He therefore published an attack on that body in *The Examiner*, an article which did him immense harm, and he was 'abused like a plague and avoided like a maniac.' Nor was this the only attack he made. He used ridicule, sarcasm and insinuations, anything that would bring them to their knees. His friends shook their heads in horror, but Haydon must speak out or die. And to show the world that he was undaunted he ordered an even larger canvas for another historical picture. He was certain that his pictures were immortal.

As a genius, too, he decided to appeal for money to two well-known men; from one he received £400 and from the other £300. There came a day, also, when the Grand Duke Nicholas of Russia visited his studio, an honour so overwhelming that Haydon almost decided to wear mustachios. But before he could commit any other rash act his health gave way and he 'shook like an aspen leaf'.

It was in 1821 that Haydon married his beloved Mary, a young widow with whom he had fallen madly in love at first sight. Indeed, the effect of love was that he could neither eat, sleep, think, write nor talk, and for the time being he hated pictures, books and even the worshipped Elgin marbles. But Mary brought him much happiness, and many children! Four of these sickened and died within a year, and the doctors declared that they had not lived because their parents were always so worried. What a tragedy!

Two years after his marriage Haydon was imprisoned for debt, and only a petition to the House of Commons set him free. Petitions, in fact, became almost a habit with him; he even bombarded the Duke of Wellington with letters on the subject of the nation's duty towards High Art. But on one matter he did compromise, for at last he condescended to paint portraits. He also took pupils and gave lectures, earning at least £1,000 a year.

Then came his great triumph (and disaster). The powers-that-be at last came round to his point of view and decided to hold a competition in order to select suitable designs for the decoration of the new Houses of Parliament. This was the moment he had waited for for forty years, and in a fever of excitement he prepared his drawings. 'A great moment has come', he wrote in his Journal, 'and I do not believe anyone so capable of wielding it as myself.' He was quite certain that he would be chosen as the chief designer, and it was the kind of work he had always longed to do—something on a big scale. But his drawings were ignominiously rejected, a most tragic blow, and he wept long and bitterly. 'I believe I am meant', he wrote to the Duke of Sutherland, 'as a human being to try the experiment how much the human brain can bear without insanity.' Shortly after, on June 22nd, 1846, he was found by his daughter stretched out before his easel with a bullet in his head and a wound in his throat. He had decided that his wife and children would be happier 'released from the burden' of his ambition. These were the last words he ever wrote:

God forgive me. Amen.
Finis of
B. R. Haydon
Stretch me no longer on this rough world.

On reading the autobiography of this strange man we are struck by one fact—that had he not been a painter he would probably have made an excellent author. This does not mean that he writes exquisite prose or that he was a profound thinker or philosopher. But he possessed several gifts which are important in an author—a genuine feeling for beauty, a passionate intensity of vision, a remarkable power of observation, and an ability to set down what he saw. In this book none of these qualities is fully developed, but had he given to writing the time and care he gave to painting the world might have gained a very fine novelist.

For instance, how vividly and well he describes people! Here are the French peasants of Dieppe—'the old women, standing with their arms across, had a gossiping, witch-like look . . . hook-nosed, snuffy, brown and wrinkled.' And here are the peasants on market day—

> dressed in a great variety of colour, white sleeves with black bracelets, rich crimson petticoats and high silvery caps. They had an old and rather overworked look, but with something extremely sweet in their manners, and a fascination in the tone of their voices.

How aptly, too, he described the Paris of that time!

> There was in everything a look of gilded slavery and bloody splendour, a tripping grace in the women, a ragged black-guardism in the men, and a polished fierceness in the soldiers . . . The remnants of Napoleons's army had a look of blasted glory, of withered pride and lurking revenge, which gave one a shudder of the sublime.

Many a fully-fledged novelist could not improve on these descriptions.

But it is Haydon's idiosyncrasies as a man which endear him to us, for this painter who was determined to quarrel with institutions and yet was so loyal and devoted to his friends is vastly entertaining. And sometimes we cannot repress a smile, for we know that the moment things go badly he will turn on the Academicians; we wait for it. And though we shake our heads—for we realise that his attacks will injure no one but himself—yet secretly we sympathise with him a little, for most of us at some time or other have written scathing letters of denunciation—and burnt them. Haydon never burnt his; only when he saw them in bold print was his honour satisfied.

His devotion to High Art, too, has something of nobility about it, for such singleness of mind is rare; most of us do not care two straws about High Art, and certainly nothing would induce us to sit drawing in a chilly vault while the heavy stones tumbled about us and we became almost frozen with cold.

His borrowings, of course, are lamentable, and we cannot defend them. Yet when we have finished his book we put it down with regret, for although we long to shake him, we feel that we have lost a friend. Never again will he be able to order 'an even larger canvas'; never again will he rejoice in the beauty of women —'the exquisite, fresh nosegay sweetness of their looks . . . the black eyes, peachy complexions, snowy necks . . . the rich crimson velvet and white satin, and lace, and muslin, and diamonds'.

He adored beauty, and he loved life with an eager, passionate zest. But life was too much for him. He was a magnificent failure.

Thomas Carlyle

1795–1881

WHEN we wander round the room of Carlyle's prim, rather elegant little house in Cheyne Row, Chelsea—it is a museum now—we find it hard to believe that this was for thirty-two years the home of that turbulent, agitated spirit. Where, we ask, is the evidence of that austere, restless, melancholy man? He could not sleep, he could not work, he was maddened by noise; his voice would thunder at the street singers and organ grinders. But here in this house all is calm and sedate; everything is neatly arranged and carefully labelled. Here is the desk at which he wrote, here is his dressing-gown, his velvet waistcoat and smoking cap. And the street outside is very quiet; scarcely a cart passes.

Then we climb up to the large attic study which was specially built to exclude noise; it is gloomy and has a small skylight. In winter, we are told, it was too cold and in summer too hot. Here he wrestled night and day with what he called his 'spiritual dragons', but all we see is a large empty room that refuses to yield up its secrets.

Indeed, the problem of Carlyle and his peculiar temperament is a fascinating one, for we never quite get to the root of it. What was the cause of his awful melancholy? Why did he never find peace? Before he died he was famous, honoured and had many devoted friends, but he was still unhappy. Perhaps, therefore, we must look to his life for an explanation.

Carlyle was the son of a village mason (an elder in the Secession Church) and he was born in a humble cottage in Ecclefechan in Scotland. Carlyle was the eldest of nine children, he was a violent-tempered and moody child, and in his fourteenth year he entered

THOMAS CARLYLE
From the drawing by Count A. D'Orsay, 1839

Edinburgh University. Like many other poor students he walked all the way, nearly a hundred miles, sleeping *en route* where he could. He was handsome, but proud, shy, sensitive and 'dreadfully in earnest'. He read unceasingly and was attracted in particular to German literature, so with the help of a grammar and dictionary he learnt German. But his years of adolescence were torture, for he was obsessed, night and day, by what he called 'the gloom of my obscure destiny'. He was conscious of exceptional intellectual power but did not know in which direction to use it. 'The future lies before me vaguely' he said. 'On the one side are obscurity and isolation, the want of all that can render life endurable. . . . Either I shall escape from this 'obscure sojourn' or perish as I ought in trying it.'

After working as a teacher of mathematics for a time—a task he heartily loathed—he accepted a post as tutor to the sons of a Mr Buller. Here he had time, also, to translate from the German the *Life of Schiller* and to write occasional articles for the *Edinburgh Review*. But writing did not come easily to him, and often he was in deep despair. Dyspepsia, also, made life a burden, and although he consulted many doctors he could find no cure. 'I want health, health, health', he cried miserably. 'My torments are greater than I am able to bear.' Sometimes he felt that death itself was imminent. 'I am well nigh done, I think. To die is hard enough at this age. To die by inches is very hard. But I *will* not. Though all things human and divine are against me I *will not*.'

His diary at this time is a record of great depression, for often he felt that all men were doomed. 'It sometimes comes on me like the shadow of death that we are all parting from one another—each moving his several, his inevitable way—fate driving us on —inexorable, dread, relentless fate. No deliverance!'

No deliverance, indeed! Life was before him, with all its wonder and interest and enchantment. But Carlyle merely withdrew more fiercely into himself. Work! Duty! Discipline! This was the meaning of life as taught him by a deeply religious mother and a stern father. 'Plain living and high thinking and hard daily labour' was the rule in his father's house.

It was at this time that he met his future wife, Jane Baillie Welsh, who was a doctor's daughter, and according to one of her admirers 'the most beautiful starry-looking creature that could be imagined'. She dressed finely, was intelligent, a good musician, a keen horsewoman and an excellent and witty conversationalist. But she was neurotic, she had a fiery Scotch temper, and she was dissatisfied with her life; vaguely she wanted to be an author. Carlyle was struck with her interest in books, and after a long correspondence he declared his devotion to her. She, however, had no desire to marry, she was not in love with him and she considered him beneath her. But after a time she realised that he was a brilliant youth with possibly a great future. She therefore accepted him, and after much trepidation on both sides they were married, living together at Craigenputtock, a very isolated Scottish farmhouse which belonged to Jane. 'How poor we were and yet how rich!' he said many years later. 'Strange how she made the desert blossom for herself and me there, what a fairy palace she had made of that wild moorland home of the poor man.' Carlyle was writing at this time *Sartor Resartus*, that ironical, impassioned document which was thought at first, by the public, to be the work of 'a literary maniac'.

But Craigenputtock ('that devil's den', as Carlyle called it) did not satisfy them for long, and after seven years they moved to Chelsea. Chelsea in those days was surrounded by green fields. There was haymaking at the proper season, and Cheyne Walk was 'a broad highway with huge shady trees, boats lying moored and a smell of shipping and tar'. On the broad river were 'white-trousered, white-shirted cockneys dashing by like arrows in their long canoes of boats'. As for the house in Cheyne Row, with its 'cunning presses', wainscoted rooms and carved staircase, it was luxury to the Carlyles. In the garden were two small vines, a walnut tree, a cherry tree and a small paved court. He liked to wander about there in dressing-gown and old straw hat, and on fine nights he would step out and smoke his final pipe there, under the stars.

But they were very poor at first, for editors would not accept his work. The public were not interested in German literature, on which he was such an authority, and his articles were dangerously controversial. He therefore decided to write a History of the French Revolution. It was a bold step, even for one of his vast reading, for although he was thirty-nine he had had little experience of life itself.

The 'birth pangs' of *The French Revolution* were agonising, for he was a comparatively inexperienced writer, and he found his material 'shapeless, dark, unmanageable' at first. He discovered, also, that he could not write unless his whole mind was 'like a furnace at white heat'. In this mood he wrote all day, and at night he would take long solitary walks.

However, the first volume was finally finished, and he lent it to John Stuart Mill to read, apparently for his opinion. Then by some awful mischance the manuscript was burnt, a tragedy that was almost 'like sentence of death' to Carlyle, as he had destroyed all his notes. Nevertheless, he took it nobly, doing his utmost to prevent Mill from realising how great was the loss.

Carlyle had met by this time most of his literary contemporaries, but for the majority of them he had the greatest contempt. 'This rascal rout, this dirty rabble', he called them. 'The very best of them are ill-natured weaklings. . . . I would only that stone walls and iron bars were constantly between us.' Byron, Shelley and Keats, of course, were dead, but his opinion of poor Keats was very unflattering. The thought of Keats, he said, made him feel sick, and reading a life of him would be like eating dead dog. Carlyle had little use, either, for Coleridge, Hazlitt or Wordsworth. Leigh Hunt, however, who was a near neighbour in Chelsea, he thought delightful at first; and Southey—who had a poor mad wife whom he refused to send to an asylum—he both liked and admired. But all such people had to give way to *The French Revolution*, which kept him in 'a fever blaze for three years'. (He always dramatized himself.) When it was finished he was in a state of 'wild excitation of nerves', he was 'solitary, weird of mood' and wished only for silence. 'How heavenly, salutary pure is silence!' he declared. 'How unattainable in the mad England that now is.'

And this dislike of noise was apparently infectious, for very soon Mrs Carlyle also complained of the same aversion. Church bells, a barking dog, a cat, a hen, a parrot, a cock, a piano; these sounds went through her 'like a sword', and her letters became one long moan about noise and headaches—present or impending—and sleeplessness. Our sympathy goes out to her, for she was delicate, but we cannot but deplore her self-pity. One cannot imagine, in fact, why she and Carlyle did not go and live at the top of the highest mountain, where there were neither cats, dogs, parrots nor church bells. But even there, alas, there would have been birds (which cannot easily be silenced) and the sighing of the wind.

The babble of aristocratic conversation, however, did not apparently affect them in the same way, for after the publication of *The French Revolution* Carlyle and his wife were lionised and entertained at most of the mansions of the rich, both in town and country. Mrs Carlyle, we are told, wore a white silk dress and white feathers in her hair, and was very insistent about her right place at table. Lord Monteagle, Lord and Lady Ashburton, the Dowager Lady Sandwich, the Duke of Argyle; these are some of the people with whom the Carlyles became acquainted. But Lord and Lady Ashburton were particularly kind. Lady Ashburton was a gifted, cultured, unconventional woman, the leader of a brilliant circle. There is no doubt that Carlyle greatly admired her, but Jane went through agonies of jealousy over this friendship, and grew angry and embittered. In vain Carlyle assured her of his entire devotion. 'Thou art dearer to me than any earthly creature', he wrote tenderly. 'I love thee always, little as thou wilt believe it.'

Indeed, his letters at this time are noble and forgiving, yet apparently she was not convinced, and became even more neurotic. Her sleeplessness became a habit, she suffered from severe nervous pains, and sometimes she sought relief in morphia. But her tears and her headaches had little effect on Carlyle, for he was far too absorbed in his work. There was a book on Cromwell to write, and one on Frederick the Great; there were pamphlets and essays on democracy, prisons, the universal vote, the rights of man, the idle rich, the condition of England, etc. On all these questions he had a great deal to say. He was no revolutionary, nor did he belong to any particular party or sect, but he had a Message and he could not rest until he had spoken. Indeed, his thoughts grew graver every year, for he believed that all nations would suffer the fate of France if they persisted in their materialistic aims. The 'hungry forties', too, had saddened him, for had he not seen that while the poor were starving the rich spent their time in shooting pheasants and amusing themselves?

So the essays were published, as he worked unceasingly, and the public listened and applauded. In his haughty, dogmatic way he scolded and lectured, and 'raved and foamed' (as Fitzgerald said), but nevertheless he commanded an audience. Why did they listen to him? Because he was passionately sincere, because his intellectual insight was quite uncanny, and because he had immense moral courage. Here was a Scottish peasant with the gift of prophecy.

As for his style, it was described as 'a wind in the orchard style that tumbled down here and there an appreciable fruit with uncouth bluster'. The truth was that he felt so strongly about everything that the words tumbled over themselves; those who have much to say care less how they say it, and his was a sort of savage genius, an untamed hurly burly of rhetoric. He had no time to polish his prose; the great thing was to get it out with all the force at his command; there could never be any serenity about Carlyle.

His conversation was very interesting, too, for even Cabinet Ministers would sit up and take notice when Carlyle held forth. He spoke with the purest Annandale accent and he did not like to be contradicted. Indeed, it was almost a waste of time, as if he was interrupted he merely shouted the louder. He did not, in fact, care whether he pleased or offended, yet he was never personal. His attacks were aimed at institutions, his century, his country. Politicians complained, of course, that he showed no insight into constitutional principles. Perhaps they were right, but nevertheless he set the trend of thought towards certain reforms, and his influence was greater than was apparent at the time.

Carlyle apparently had his softer side, too, and at the splendid soirées of Lady Blessington he was listened to as an oracle. Society women thought him the oddest creature, with his dark hair, lined brow, rosy cheeks and perpetual pipe. His rich and quaint philosophy would come pouring out in a copious stream, and in the company of ladies he laughed heartily. There was something 'too too whimsical' about his earnestness, his simplicity and his mild yet derisive scorn.

Mrs Carlyle accompanied him to these parties whenever possible, but her health did not improve, and often he went alone. 'It is very brilliant, all at Addiscombe' (Lady Ashburton's), he wrote; 'wealth in abundance, ruled over by grace in abundance.' There is no doubt that the wealth and the grace dazzled him, and that the patronage of such people was extremely pleasant. Indeed, Lady Ashburton's kindness exceeded his expectations, for she presented him with a fine black horse. Every evening, therefore, he could be seen, after sunset, riding out towards the country— all alone, of course. His thoughts were still melancholy, but at least he no longer pondered on the gloom of his obscure destiny. He was a famous man. When he returned home he would go into the drawing-room, where Mrs Carlyle sat by the fire with the candles lit. She, poor thing, would tell him all the news of the day—how the maid had got drunk, or flown into a temper, how she had discovered bugs in the beds, how Mr Tennyson had been to call, how the maid's mattress 'was being eaten from under her with moths', how Mrs Leigh Hunt had again sent her servant round to borrow a little tea, or a pair of irons, or a few teaspoons, or a steel fender (Mrs Leigh Hunt was a great borrower); how the young lady next door had been practising all day on the piano (quite unbearable!) and the hens next door had been cackling and shrieking like demons. . . . Carlyle was devoted to her in his way ('She flickered round me like perpetual radiance', he said), but ill-health had already destroyed her good looks, she was often difficult, and if he appeared to neglect her for his work, there was really no help for it.

Then, quite suddenly, in 1866, Mrs Carlyle died. She was driving alone in her brougham in Kensington Gardens, and the coachman was not aware that anything was wrong until suddenly he looked round; and there she was with her hands folded, quite dead. Carlyle was away at the time and it was a great shock to him. In fact he was not able to bring himself to write a sketch of her life until three years later, and then he found the task too painful, and merely left a few notes. But these notes have a very real beauty, for Carlyle was at his best when recalling the past. 'Why is the past so beautiful?' he demanded. He also wrote memoirs of his friends—Lord Jeffrey, Edward Irving and Sterling; all were admirable, as he had a wonderful memory and could write of his friends with great tenderness.

The latter years of Carlyle's life were lonely and rather wearisome. Life was a strange, restless dream, and sometimes death seemed welcome. 'Be wise, all ye living', he said, 'and remember that time passes and will not return.' But he had many good friends—Tennyson, Emerson, Ruskin, Browning, and with Emerson in particular he spent many pleasant hours; they even made a pilgrimage together to Stonehenge. Beneath those towering stones they talked of Philosophy, History and Science, of the fate of man, and the origin of this awe-inspiring monument. But it was Carlyle who provided the gloomy summing-up: 'In these days', he said, 'it would become an architect to consult only the grim necessity and say "I can build you a coffin for such dead persons as you are and for such dead purposes as you have, but you shall have no ornament".' This, then, was what he thought of his fellow-countrymen; and even in that delightful spot, high up on Salisbury Plain, with wild flowers at his feet and larks singing overhead, he was not happy, nor did he apparently see any hope for the future. He added later, as the light began to fade—for they sat there till twilight—'I plant cypresses wherever I go, and if I am in search of pain I cannot go wrong.'

Yet gloomy as he was, there was now no lack of appreciation

of his work, for he was awarded the Prussian Order of Merit and offered (by Disraeli) the Grand Cross of the Bath and a pension. The English awards he refused, but he was gratified, nevertheless. He died at the age of eighty-five and was buried at Ecclefechan.

So what shall we say of Carlyle? That he was a fine historian, a good critic and a great thinker. For the serious-minded and the student of history he offers a grand feast. His historical workmanship is extremely sound, and although his style is abrupt, mannered and ungainly, it is graphic and vigorous, and his power to describe a scene and character vividly and with atmosphere is undeniable. As for his feeling for beauty, he did not notice the coming of the first crocus or the diamond dew on the thorn; he noticed only the storm gathering, the sky darkening and the blood-red sunset. As a verse-making poet he failed—it was not his métier—but he certainly enriched English poetry and prose by revealing a whole new world of imagination and artistic treatment in German literature. With all its faults German literature was a great revelation to the English literary world at that time. There is no doubt, also, that Carlyle shed a new light on the art of criticism; he showed us what the real function of the critic should be.

The only serious fault we have to find with him, in fact, is in the tone of the essays; he is the serious, opinionated schoolmaster who gives us credit for nothing. He is determined to take us through every stage of his argument—a most irritating trait— for we feel that having pointed the way in no uncertain manner we really do not need leading by the hand on the entire journey. Yet his essays will always be interesting, quite apart from their subject matter, to the student of human nature, for there his character and the whole background of his life are reflected—the rugged simplicity, earnestness, integrity and pugnaciousness of his father, the deep piety of his mother, the austerity and poverty and dourness of that Scottish home. We can so well believe that he hated contradiction, and we are not in the least surprised that his work made him irritable, sleepless and melancholy. Indeed, as

166

we read his books we seem to be living in a perpetual thunder-storm. The sky, of course, clears occasionally and the light comes through the clouds; sometimes there is even a rainbow. But this is Carlyle, and here, surely, is poetry. The books are the man him-self, revealed as if by his own brilliant lightning.

As for Mrs Carlyle, she too has made a contribution to literature, for her letters give an authentic picture of the life and outlook of a woman of her day. It was the age of candle-light and magni-ficent parties, dark streets, no bathrooms (even in the finest houses), appalling slums, frightful infant mortality and cruelty to children. Men wore neckcloths or cravats, train journeys were made in open carriages, and only about fifty per cent of the working classes could read and write. It was the day of improving and serious conversation and elegant manners; and tea, coffee and sugar were luxuries to be locked up every night with the silver. This was Mrs Carlyle's world, and in pondering on her life we remember all sorts of odd things about her—that she kept a leech as a pet, that as a tiny child she was given a sip from her mother's glass and said, 'Mamma, wine makes cosy'—a charming re-mark. We think of her sitting in her little drawing-room singing old Scotch songs to the elegant Leigh Hunt, and we remember that she once found a lost child—she had none of her own—who said, 'I had a pretty brother and they put him in a pretty coffin.' Last of all we see her sitting at grand parties surrounded by peers, cabinet ministers and bejewelled women, and we feel a little sad, for we know that she felt out of place, that she had really been invited because she was the wife of the celebrated author, Carlyle.

Ivan Turgenev
1818–1883

SPASKOE, the large Russian country house where Turgenev spent his youth, has probably been pulled down long ago, but even if it still stands, the splendour and the feasting and the tyranny have gone for ever. Haunted by ghosts it may be, for how the serf-girls wept when marriage and love were denied them! And how the men groaned when they were whipped! But that is long ago; the days of serfdom have passed, and it was Turgenev himself who played such a great part in the emancipation of the serfs in Russia. By his works he laid bare in all its aspects the tyranny of serfdom, and in doing so he interpreted to Europeans the soul of Russia, a country which at that time was almost untouched by civilisation.

It is not easy for English readers to picture a Russian household of the early nineteenth century, for its regime has no counterpart in any English household of the same period. Spaskoe was a spacious wooden mansion, and Madame Turgenev, the wealthy owner, possessed five thousand serfs—her household staff alone numbered forty—but they were all liable at any moment to be lashed across the face, or cruelly beaten or sold. Madame Turgenev was determined to be obeyed, ritually and absolutely, almost as though she were the Emperor. She gloried in the feeling of power, and she exercised the privilege of thrashing the serfs with her own hands. Her family fared little better, for a young ward was nearly driven to suicide, while Ivan, her favourite son, was thrashed almost every day. One could discuss nothing with this imperious woman, yet she spent hours in her private chapel, praying, and crossing herself continually. She was unhappy, for

IVAN TURGENEV

her handsome soldier husband was consistently unfaithful—some of his bastard children were in her employ—and she herself had been ill-treated by her stepfather in her youth.

But when it pleased her to be gay, the great rooms would be thrown open to her neighbours, and under the glittering chandeliers the tables would be set with rich food and wines. There would be a display of fireworks, and the guests would dance till morning. Sometimes a play was performed, too, in the private theatre, the serfs themselves becoming the actors and musicians. It was the day of 'wigs, canes, perfumes, snuff-boxes and embroidered coats', and life was leisurely, at least for the rich.

In those days in Russia few had ever thought of criticising the old order; a slave was a slave; he was not fit to be anything else. But long before Ivan Turgenev reached manhood the whole regime of his mother's household had become distasteful to this sensitive boy. That many of the serfs were idle, drunken, dishonest and dirty he realised, but he saw also how uncomplainingly they shouldered their burdens, how silently they bore with insults and how nobly they died. 'It is my hour', they would murmur resignedly.

How miserably they lived, too, in the villages! Their huts, generally covered by a rotting thatch, were gloomy, smoky, ill-drained and ill-ventilated, and their clothing was of the poorest description. In the bitter winters they suffered terribly; a blizzard would sweep over the countryside, and the very birds would freeze in the air, but life and work must still go on. Only the strongest survived, and the condition of the children was often pitiful. It was a vast complicated problem. But Madame Turgenev saw no problem, and had her son expressed his views he would have been dismissed from her presence in a storm of anger.

Ivan was a handsome youth, tall, fair and blue-eyed. Is it strange, then, that the serf-girls admired him and even lay in wait for him? He was lonely, and snatched at any consolation that offered itself. So passion came to him early and it was in the garden at Spaskoe that a young serf-girl beckoned him with love in her eyes. But beauty too—and trees in particular—enchanted him; he could not see without emotion 'a branch covered with foliage outlined against the sky', and often at night he would lie for hours under a big, sweet-scented lime, listening to the nightingales. His thoughts were confused, strange, melancholy, and he craved for intellectual companionship. To whom could he turn? There were the foreign governesses and tutors engaged by his mother to teach him, but with these people he had little in common.

At Petersburg University, however, he heard fine talk indeed. Sitting over the samovar late into the night the students discussed —as is the way with Russians—the whole future of the human race. They were burning with enthusiasms, high visions and passionate aspirations; they were often angry and indignant too, for the need for reform in their country was very great. Where, except in Russia, were there so many frustrations, injustices and evils? The political fabric was rotten through and through, bribery and corruption were rife, the Press was heavily censored, and the Law Courts were almost a farce. And the first step towards remedying these evils was, of course, the emancipation of the serfs; nothing could be achieved until the masses had gained their freedom. But the Government had forbidden all public discussion on the subject; they believed that if the serfs were freed they would kick over the traces and wallow in anarchy. Discussion, therefore, took place in secret, and finally this burning desire for freedom began to express itself in a strong, original literature that commanded an ever-growing audience. On the young Turgenev it made a most powerful impression. Yet what contribution could he make towards this movement? He was not by nature a revolutionary; he was too gentle, too polished. Finally in spite of his mother's scorn (for a noble, surely, ought to 'serve the Tsar and make a career and a name for himself in the army') he decided to become an author.

Our first glimpse of him in this role is in France, where we see him at the fine chateau which belonged to Madame Pauline Viardot, the prima donna. Courtavenal was a picturesque castle with drawbridge, turrets and moat, surrounded by meadows and woods; and here he wrote his first book, *The Annals of a Sportsman*. He had fled from his native country because everything in Russia distressed him and filled him with indignation and scorn. 'I had either to submit, to walk meekly in the common rut, the beaten path, or tear myself away with one wrench. . . . I chose the latter course.' he said. But there was another reason for his flight; he was already deeply in love with Pauline Viardot. He had loved her from the moment of their first meeting in Petersburg (before her marriage) and although, of course, his passion was hopeless, nevertheless he followed her like a shadow. People might gossip—as indeed they did—yet neither he nor she cared.

The prima donna was not beautiful, but she had great charm, and she was a supreme artist. Was it not Charles Dickens, who on hearing her sing in Paris, wept so profusely that M. Viardot was obliged to introduce him with the remark, 'Permit me to present a fountain'? Her influence over Turgenev was, of course, profound, and she certainly contributed to that culture, that exquisite sophistication which so characterised him as a man. 'To dine with Turgenev was to dine with Europe', it was said.

So here was this young aristocrat, living in France, yet writing articles and books almost entirely about Russia. Indeed, there was his heart; he had but to close his eyes and he was back again tramping through the green woods, driving along the hot, sunlit plains, calling at a country house, watching the peasants carting rye, standing amidst the dust and din of a horse fair. But it was chiefly the peasants who came so vividly before his eyes. What indeed could be more exquisite than the best type of peasant girl:

The door was softly opened, and I caught sight of a tall and slender girl of twenty, with a dark, gypsy face, golden-brown eyes, and hair as black as pitch; her large white teeth gleamed between full red lips. She had on a white dress. A blue shawl pinned close round her throat with a gold brooch, half hid her slender beautiful arms, in which one could see the fineness of her race. She took two steps with the bashful awkwardness of some wild creature, stood still and looked down. . . .

There were so many beautiful girls in Russia. His mind was haunted, too, by memories of the steppe, where on his long hunting and shooting trips he had spent many wonderful days:

It is time to turn homewards to the village, to the hut where you will stay the night. . . . Meanwhile, the night comes on. . . . Over there above the black bushes, there is a vague brightness on the horizon. . . . What is it? A fire? . . . No, it is the moon rising. And away below, to the right, the village lights are twinkling already. . . . And here at last is your hut. Through the tiny window you see a table, with a white cloth, a candle burning, supper. . . .

As for the tragic question of serfdom, surely he could set down what he had seen—the cruelty and the misery! Surely he could make his contribution to the great movement that had been started! These people must be freed; he would never rest until it was accomplished. And yet, how difficult it was to write this book! It was agonising. He would walk up and down his room 'groaning like a lion in his cage'. Yet in the end it was finished, and to his amazement the book was received with enthusiasm in Russia; he was acclaimed as a young author of genuine talent. But most of all was his book welcomed by the ardent advocates of emancipation, for here was a picture of serfdom written with an irony that was even more effective than bitterness or anger.

It was not to be supposed, however, that the book would escape the eyes of the Government, for in a way it was propaganda disguised as fiction, yet they could hardly suppress it. They waited, therefore, for two years, and then, when Turgenev had the courage to refer to Gogol (in a letter to the Press) as 'a great man' the Government gave their orders and Turgenev was arrested. He was imprisoned for a month, and later on was ordered to live only at Spaskoe, and refused permission to go abroad.

What anguish it was to be parted from his beloved prima donna! Letters were a very poor consolation. 'You know that I belong to you wholly and for ever' he wrote. 'I should like to lay my whole life as a carpet beneath your beloved feet.' When, when would they meet again?

It was, in fact, four years before he was allowed to leave Russia, and then, when the Viardots moved to England for a time, Turgenev accompanied them. Here he was graciously received in literary circles. He shot grouse in Scotland—Robert Browning was of the party—he met Carlyle, Disraeli, Thackeray and Macaulay, and he was entertained at Pembroke College, Oxford, where he received an honorary degree. With his commanding height, his charm and his 'look of power' he made an excellent impression.

But finally the party returned to France and settled at Bougival near Paris, where Turgenev bought a very fine house with spacious grounds and a river view. Here the Viardots were near neighbours. Spaskoe, however, still belonged to Turgenev—he had inherited it from his mother—and his visits to Russia, therefore, were fairly regular. But with every visit the beauty of the place seemed to increase. The property was deteriorating, it is true, as it was badly managed, and the gardens were always neglected. But the swans still floated serenely on the lake, the tall rye waved as before in the surrounding fields, and the nightingales and orioles still sang. The peasants pleased him, too, for on fête days they would crowd on to the terrace and sing songs under his window. On the other hand, the big empty house, with its creaking, neglected furniture, its long corridors and the curtains rustling in empty rooms, saddened him. The place, of course, needed a woman, but marriage for him was out of the question. It was merely 'a cruel irony' he declared. And if matters on the estate were not as they should be—for the peasants robbed him right and left—what could he do? He was engrossed in his writing, and he had never been able to assert himself.

In the meantime, he was literally besieged by beggars—former servants, cripples, the blind, the unfortunate. His heart went out to them all, but there was a limit to his purse.

One needed the society, too, at times, of one's fellow authors, although they were a difficult lot, and apparently as jealous as pigeons. They quarrelled bitterly, and he was always being dragged into their disputes. How he despised, also, the endless talk and shilly-shallying of his political associates! He himself was incapable of literary jealousy, yet somehow he fell foul of his contemporaries, and with Dostoevsky friendly relations became quite impossible. 'He is failing', cried Dostoevsky triumphantly, when *Lear of the Steppes* was published. 'He is becoming paler and paler.'

Tolstoy also proved a difficult friend, for with his strong views he could not keep silent even on matters which did not concern him. He was, for instance, extremely tactless regarding the education of Turgenev's daughter, Pauline. This child was the result of a liaison between Turgenev and a serf-girl named Fetiska, whom he had purchased (in spite of his views on serf-dom!) from his cousin Elizabeth, after much bargaining, for the sum of seven hundred roubles. The value of a serf-girl at that time was merely fifty roubles, so there had been something specially appealing about Fetiska. She was not beautiful, however, but her soft, dark eyes, wistful expression and slender graceful figure had touched some chord in his heart. He wanted her, he intended to have her, and finally he had taken her to Spaskoe, where he had lived in retirement with her for about a year. He had tried to teach her to read, but without success. Fetiska, poor child, had not held his affection for long, but he was devoted to Pauline, the daughter of this strange union. He was proud of her and was anxious that she should be well educated. When he and Tolstoy were dining together one evening, therefore, the matter was discussed, but Turgenev became so enraged at Tolstoy's remarks on the subject that he lost all patience and shouted, 'Be silent, Tolstoy, or I will throw my fork at you'. The result was very nearly a duel, but in the end the affair was patched up.

Tolstoy was at this time a most irritating and priggish young man, who had formed the habit of always taking the opposite view of any opinion expressed. He was apparently determined to be regarded as a man of original thought—as indeed he was—but this trait made him unpopular. He was also continually sending challenges to duels in order to vindicate his 'honour'. As a rule, however, his challenges were ignored.

It was sad that the two authors could not agree, as Turgenev genuinely admired Tolstoy's work. 'When this young wine ripens', he said, 'it will be a drink fit for the gods.' Tolstoy, however, was intensely irritated by Turgenev's moderation concerning Russia's problems, insisting that it was mere indifference.

But Russia could never hold Turgenev for long; there was always that aching desire for France and his beloved Pauline Viardot. How he suffered over this attachment! He was like a bird caught in a net, and he knew that to the day of his death he would never be able to free himself. Indeed, early in the year of 1857 he passed through a period of terrible darkness, owing to a breach between the singer and himself which seemed irreparable; he was in bodily and spiritual anguish, and according to Tolstoy 'a pitiful sight'. The truth was that a woman's love was essential to him because in his unhappy childhood he had never known a mother's love. Finally he went back to Madame Viardot, only to be humiliated there, and tormented by the doubt as to whether he or Pauline's new lover was the father of her baby.

In the end Turgenev tore himself away and went to Italy, sick in mind and body. He believed that he would never write again, although he was not yet thirty-nine. He was finished . . . finished. . . . Yet this crisis proved to be the turning point in his life, and soon he was able to start another book. Then a few years later, to his great joy, the emancipation of the serfs became an established fact; the great cause had triumphed. Many problems remained, it is true, so his work was not finished.

We cannot remember Turgenev's old age without sadness, for was ever man so lonely? 'There cannot be artists who are actually happy', he said, 'for happiness is repose, and repose creates nothing.' He had achieved fame, but it meant very little to him. His health had deteriorated; his heart was failing, and he suffered severely from gout, an affliction that put an end to his shooting and the long hunting trips he had always enjoyed so much in the past. His bay mare, Queen Victoria, often stood idle in her stable for weeks at a time. His daughter was now married, and his great friend, Flaubert, had lately died. As for his love affairs—he had had so many—they had quite lost their flavour. Secretly he longed for a wife and a real home, but it was too late. Life had slipped by like a flash and already he was over sixty. His world, indeed, seemed to be falling to pieces and he declared that in his soul there was 'a darkness blacker than night. The days pass like an instant, empty, aimless, colourless . . . One has no more right to life, no more desire to live. . . . Oh, my friend,' he wrote, 'we are the vibrations of a vase broken long ago.' Yet his disillusionment did not embitter him. He still believed in the young, and aspiring authors who came to him daily, begging for advice and help, were assisted by every means in his power: he devoted endless time to their problems.

Towards the end of his life Turgenev suffered a great deal, and finally he declared to his old friend Charcot that he was being pursued by Assyrian soldiers. Such confusion of mind did not last, however, and he died in Pauline Viardot's commanding presence on 3rd December, 1883, and as he had wished, his journal was burnt in the garden at Bougival. A public funeral was suggested, but the Russian Government refused to allow it; they had feared his power in life; they feared it in death, too. Yet his task was done. 'My one desire for my tomb', he said, 'is that they shall engrave upon it what my book has accomplished for the emancipation of the serfs'.

It can be said, indeed, that Turgenev's contribution to the cause of freedom and justice in Russia was a very real one, for through *The Annals of a Sportsman* he accomplished for the Russian serf what the author of *Uncle Tom's Cabin* achieved for the American slave. The Russian novelist was the only voice that could speak for Russia, and even these brave men had to pay the penalty, for with every line they wrote they risked imprisonment and banishment. And if their courage is questioned because they were not more active as revolutionaries, if it is said that they did not act but merely spoke, the answer is that as artists they could only behave according to their kind. Besides, is not the written word more powerful than the sword?

It was Turgenev, too, who through his books interpreted Russia to western Europe, in terms of the west, and he brought to his work the vision of an artist, the most delicate responsiveness, the warmest heart, and the clearest vision. As a cosmopolitan he was able to see Russia from both inside and out, and therein lay his great asset—a perfect detachment. He was obviously no fanatic, but he wrote with a moderation that will always command a more rational audience than a passionate conviction.

Turgenev's books have also had a far-reaching influence on literature itself, for his method of lyrical impressionism—a method that was unique at the time—has inspired a whole generation of writers. There are no striking lines or colours in his books, yet he can create with marvellous skill that strange, elusive thing, atmosphere. No one can express the 'moods' of life better than Turgenev. And with what fine discrimination, too, he portrays character! The young Russian girl, naïve, fresh, simple, devoted and single-minded, is always beautifully drawn. She has courage, a high sense of duty and a wonderful power of passive resistance. These are his heroines, and they personify the noble spirit of self-sacrifice shown by so many young Russian women in their fight against tyranny. It was they who worked and planned for Russia, often under the most dangerous conditions.

There is, however, another quality in Turgenev's books for which we are extremely grateful—his power to portray the enchantment of love. All his love stories are exquisitely fresh, tender, poignant, and they are told with serenity and charm. His sympathy does not intrude—for that is not the Russian way—but it is gently and beautifully implied. It extends in particular to lovers, but also to those whom life has treated badly—the superfluous, the unsuccessful. It does not matter to Turgenev whether you are a noble or a tramp, a princess or a peasant girl; he is watching and admiring; he does not condemn or get a cheap laugh at your expense, he has no particular desire even to analyse you or watch your reactions; he merely wishes to understand, to hold out a hand of sympathy.

But we cannot leave him without remembering in particular that great novel *Fathers and Children*, published in 1862. Here is a book which is deeply significant of one of the most profound changes in thought that mankind has ever had to face—the change from a world dominated by Faith to a world of Science. Bazarov, the chief figure in this moving book, is a provincial doctor. Brilliant, original and of strong personality, yet ruthlessly outspoken, he is the very symbol of that young generation who with the coming of science fought courageously against the superstitions, illusions, hypocrisies and sentimentalities of the past. Bazarov is intensely egotistical and revolutionary in thought; there is none of that inaction about him which is the vice of the Russian temperament; he wishes to see nature stripped of all ideals, traditions and ancient beliefs, and even love and duty must be sacrified to this end. He does not believe in art or poetry—for that is merely Nature's glamour—and he cares nothing for honours, success, praise or blame; he is the ardent seeker after truth. There is something extremely fine about this brave young enthusiast who believes that science will in time control nature. Yet finally nature herself takes charge; Bazarov cuts himself in dissecting a corpse and becomes infected. The district doctor has no caustic, and Bazarov dies; science cannot save him. . . . He had meant to bring to Russia a new spirit and a new hope, yet his life comes to an end in a stupid way; the ignorance and apathy of the old Russia has triumphed over the scientist.

Let us confess, without shame, that we cannot read of Bazarov's death without being moved to tears. 'I'd break down so many things', he says, as he is dying. 'There were problems to solve and I was a giant.' But already his eyes are closing. . . . And yet with what a fine glow he has lighted up the surrounding darkness! He has blazed across the night like a meteor, and disappeared, leaving no trace. We have all met Bazarov; he is not merely a Russian product. He and his kind, young pioneers of scientific thought, have made their own contribution to civilisation, often unheard and unsung; their indomitable courage, their honesty, their love of truth, are infinitely inspiring, and no one has told their story more finely than Turgenev.

Fëdor Dostoevsky

1822–1881

HAD one been invited to a literary gathering in Petersburg in the early 70's one might have observed a short elderly man, bearded, gaunt, pale, intensely nervous, a man whose face bore the marks of great suffering. It would have been difficult to distinguish him from a peasant, for even his clothes were a little odd. His faded hair was brushed back from hollow temples and a wrinkled forehead, his mouth drooped, his face twitched unpleasantly. Certainly one would have hesitated to talk to him, for there was something quite repellent about that mournful old man. But on enquiring from one's neighbour, possibly the charming Turgenev, one would have been told that that was the distinguished author Dostoevsky.

And, indeed, how his looks belied him! For those eyes, apparently so sad and meek, could flash and burn with the fire of genius, and even five minutes' conversation was sufficient to show that he was a vital and magnetic personality. Turgenev has described him as 'wicked, envious and vicious', and according to one critic he was 'the most evil Christian he had ever met', yet Dostoevsky's second wife declared that he was 'the purest being on earth'. The facts are, of course, that all these descriptions are true, for he was a divided personality and this fierce conflict of mind and spirit was the theme, and indeed the motive power behind all his work. He was both evil and pure, mean and noble, intensely egotistical yet moved by a tender sympathy for the unfortunate and a genuine passion for the liberties of mankind.

Externals did not interest Dostoevsky; he was concerned merely with the soul. He himself had sounded every note on that vast organ; he knew all the stops, he was familiar with every chord. As a prisoner in Siberia he had seen the souls of men stripped bare and revealed in all their savagery and nobility. He had been in company with men who had suffered intensely in a living hell, where pretence was useless, where fine manners counted for nothing, where hope was dead. And from this he had emerged with one conviction—that 'love is the whole world, the most precious of jewels'. It was, in fact, love which redeemed Dostoevsky, and that is why, to his own wife, he was the purest being on earth.

But it is impossible to understand this strange, complex character without recalling to mind again his early environment and the facts of his life. He was born in Moscow (on 30th October, 1821), the son of a well-born, but miserly, drunken and ill-tempered surgeon who seventeen years later was murdered by his own serfs in revenge for his cruelty. But Dostoevsky's youth was spent in Petersburg, a city which apparently stirred his imagination deeply. The magnificent buildings and churches, the gilded palaces, the river Neva glowing in the light of the evening sun, the beggars' bonfires, the pall of smoke lying across the dark blue sky; all this appeared to him as 'a fantastic, magical vision'. But he was poor, and life was drab. At the College of Military Engineering, where he completed his education, he was quite unable to compete socially with his richer companions and he was often deeply humiliated. Also, he was an epileptic, an affliction that frequently brought him to shame. When, therefore, he began to write, the praise he received went quite to his head. 'Everybody looks upon me as a wonder of the world', he said.

He lived, we gather, mostly in dreary rooms in the poor quarter of the city. We see the characters in his early books, therefore, haunting the lamp-lit pavements, the dark alley-ways of lodging-houses, the doorways of churches, the shabby lounges of cheap restaurants. These people do not move in a world of beauty, but come and go like sinister shadows in the dusk. Nevertheless, we see them very clearly; at times they are revealed as if by a sudden flash of lightning, and only when Dostoevsky has finished does

FËDOR DOSTOEVSKY
From the painting by V. G. Perov, 1878

the darkness completely close round them again. They seem cut
off from life, wrapped in their own sad bewilderment. Indeed,
there is no doubt that most of Dostoevsky's characters are utterly
bewildered; they are constantly at war with themselves. Whether
they are landladies, clerks, pawnbrokers, valets, governesses,
misers, drunkards, prostitutes, young girls or generals, princes,
princesses, landowners or priests, they are queer folk; yet how
deeply interesting they become under his pen!

But if Dostoevsky had little eye for beauty in nature, he never
failed to see beauty in women. They, at least, assume an air of
loveliness the moment he begins to speak of them:

> . . . she might have been twenty. Marvellously beautiful and
> dressed in a jacket of some rich, dark, glossy fur, with a
> white satin scarf tied over her head and knotted under her
> chin, she walked with her eyes cast down and a sort of
> meditative gravity on her face which imparted to the tender,
> gentle lines of her child-like countenance a sort of clear-cut
> yet mournful air . . .

It was love, of course, which created the bright halo. And who
can say how many love affairs Dostoevsky had? They were
fantastic, chaotic; they tossed him up and down like a feather in
the wind and left him in utter despair. There is no doubt that his
life was extremely disorderly. But even as he sowed his wild oats
tragedy was approaching, for in 1849, as a result of his political
activities, he was arrested and imprisoned in a dungeon. Eight
months elapsed before he was tried, and finally he and his companions were conveyed to a public square, set before a scaffold
and prepared for execution. The death sentence was read, and a
dagger was broken over their heads. Only at the very last moment
were they reprieved, and finally transported in chains to Siberia,
where in the company of thieves, murderers and other vicious
criminals Dostoevsky spent four terrible years. His hardships—
which he has described in masterly fashion—changed his whole
attitude to life, and all his ideas of good and evil, for although he

was disgusted with his companions and remained aloof, nevertheless he studied them unceasingly and was surprised to discover that some of the most hardened criminals had 'deep, strong, beautiful natures' which had deteriorated, often because circumstances had proved too strong for them.

Thus, from this chaotic beginning emerges Dostoevsky the novelist, warped to a certain extent in mind and body, but with a spirit unbroken, and with an insight into the human soul so profound that it can only be likened to clairvoyance. And this amazing power developed rapidly, until it was plain that here was a genius of the very highest order. It is, indeed, an astonishing faculty, this unearthing of layer after layer of human consciousness, until we come down to the very springs of human behaviour. But to say that it is disturbing is an understatement; it shakes us to the very roots of our being. This, of course, is why few of us can read his books for any length of time; we are fascinated but nevertheless repelled. And is there not also a dark undercurrent of evil swirling through the deep waters, something which is so terrifying that often we are obliged to put the book aside for a time? We return to it again, of course, for the appeal of Dostoevsky is irresistible. He puts to shame all those complacent authors who have endeavoured to interest us in the past. They fade away to mere 'match-stick men' and the people of whom they write seem like stuffed dolls bowing and posturing. As for the lives of the poor, which Dostoevsky has described so powerfully and yet tenderly, here we are living in a new world. We, who have never heard children wailing for food or seen a beautiful girl forced on to the streets from poverty, know now that these things have really happened. We know and we are roused to pity and anger.

Thus does Dostoevsky shake us from our complacency and at the same time enthrall and disturb us. And we realise without a shadow of doubt that he speaks from bitter experience. We remember how, during his exile in Europe, whence he had fled to escape his many creditors in Russia (alas, his financial affairs were always in confusion), that he lived in the most wretched poverty. We remember how, one winter's day, when the snow was falling, he was forced to pawn even his 'pantaloons' and his young wife's last warm woollen garments, although she was suckling her baby. We remember, too (and we cannot bear to blame him), that he endeavoured to mend matters by gambling wildly, day after day, staking and losing even his wife's savings. We remember that finally his beloved child died. So when he describes some unfortunate man who is weak and irresponsible, yet has a secret craving for a more worthy and dignified life, we are moved to pity for Dostoevsky himself; he had inherited evil tendencies, and although he desired passionately to do what was right, he did not always succeed. His life was one long inner conflict, the struggle between the flesh and the spirit. 'If, when I was a child, I had been blessed with parents I should never have become what I am to-day.' he said. He was severely handicapped, too, by the mental disturbance caused by his epileptic fits. Before the fits he experienced the strangest and most wonderful exaltation, a joy so intense that it was almost unbearable, but when the fit had passed he was haunted by a terrible feeling of guilt, and a fear that he had committed some dreadful crime. Nevertheless, whatever his mood, he was forced to write in order to live, and he wrote night and day, hurriedly, frantically, with his brain 'always at boiling point'. He was constantly working against time in order to pay off his debts. He was unhappy, too, away from Russia and longed to return. 'I need Russia for my life, my work', he declared passionately.

But what strikes us as perhaps the strangest fact about Dostoevsky is that in spite of his unhappy experiences, in spite of all the evil he had seen and the injustice of life in Russia, there is no bitterness or cynicism in his outlook. Nor does he attempt to find a scapegoat or lay about him with a whip on any social class or system. He does not try even to sum up the result of his observations or to preach; nor can he be described as a pessimist. The reason is, of course, that he was a genuine artist; he divined without reasoning, believed without analysing; he had the gift of the seer and he never allowed his vision to be cluttered up with ambiguities. For this we are eternally grateful.

We are in fact grateful to Dostoevsky for so many things that to name one or two seems inadequate. We remember, however, in particular his delightful study of boys in *The Brothers Karamazov*, his moving portrait of a wise simpleton in *The Idiot* and his two wonderful stories *The Gentle Maiden* and *Apropos of the Falling Sleet*. We are deeply grateful, also, for his power to show us, as few other writers have done, how strangely good and evil are intermingled in men and women. But most of all we are indebted to him for his magnificent presentation of the life of the Russia of his time. Here we can feel the throbbing heart of that vast passionate, unhappy, restless country. It is a picture that is shot through and through with a savage, poetic beauty, not the beauty of scene (for Dostoevsky rarely attempts to fill in the surroundings or create any strong atmosphere for his characters; they seem to create their own), but the beauty of the soul's yearnings. We feel indeed, that he was far too agitated with his own tremendous conflicts to notice whether the snow was blowing in at the door, or the wind shaking the treetops, or the sun beating down upon his head. Time, too, in his stories often seems to hang suspended. It does not really stretch between lunch and dinner or sleeping and waking, but between brooding and action.

So as we ponder on the man himself as revealed in his life and his work, we come to the conclusion that his pursuit of happiness was an extremely painful process. We are thankful, therefore, that he achieved before he died some measure of peace and success. His second marriage, to a young and sensible stenographer, was a happy one, and the success of his books finally released him from poverty. His speech at the Pushkin celebrations, too, was a great triumph. He died, however, a few months later, aged nearly sixty, but such was his remarkable vitality that he had already planned another great book. There was apparently no rest for Dostoevsky, except in the grave.

As for his influence on modern writers, it cannot really be measured, for he was the first European novelist to explore the soul of man and make it a part of literature, and although hundreds of authors have since attempted to tread the same path with varying success, he still remains supreme in his own line. He added to the novel, in fact, a new dimension, and if at the same time he broke away from the old forms, it is because they were inadequate for his purpose; he had too much to say.

There are, of course, many irritating faults in his books; he exaggerates, he creates involved and absurd plots, he sometimes becomes melodramatic, he digresses and repeats himself. But we forgive all this because his achievement is so great; of that there can be no doubt whatever.

Yet we cannot discuss Dostoevsky without also considering his influence on the Russian politics of the time, for there can be no doubt that in turn he influenced various schools of thought. His first book, *Poor People*, was hailed by the radical intelligentsia (who were seething with revolt against the conditions in Russia under the rule of Nicholas I) as a wonderful piece of propaganda for their cause. For at this time Dostoevsky was an earnest disciple of Belinsky, who had taught him to reject the Christian foundations of our society, and to believe that religion, family property, nationalism and patriotism were criminal. Dostoevsky did, indeed, take part in a plot to excite the peasants to an open revolt against serfdom (though this fact was not revealed until many years later). It is strange, however, that after spending four years in a convicts' prison Dostoevsky became a passionate critic of radical liberalism and an enemy of revolution. It was a very puzzling change of heart, but Dostoevsky's explanation was that by coming into closer contact with the common people of Russia he was converted to their simple faith, which, he maintained, preserved the basic truth of Christianity in its purest form, uncorrupted by western ideas. Actually, however, the account which Dostoevsky gives of his life in Siberia in *Notes from the House of the Dead* is not a revelation of a new faith and a new philosophy; it is merely a revelation of the experience of mass suffering. His revolutionary friends had taught him that social evils were not due to vice and moral deficiency but were the result of political and economical conditions. They regarded moral depravity as a mere consequence of environment, of unequal opportunities for self-fulfilment, and of maldistribution of wealth. Dostoevsky's experiences in Siberia gave the lie to this theory, and he realised that Belinsky had misled him when he claimed that the Russians were the most atheistic of all nations. Finally, therefore, Dostoevsky rejected outright the principles of liberal reform and social revolution. And in setting out his later views he did, indeed, prove himself a prophet:

> I maintain (he said) that if all these modern sublime teachers were given ample opportunity to destroy the old society and to build it anew, there would result such darkness, such chaos, something so coarse, so blind, so inhuman, that the entire edifice would crumble away, to the accompaniment of the maledictions of mankind even before its erection had been completed.

He considered that this was what the renunciation of Christ would lead to, and he may yet be proved abundantly right.

Count Leo Tolstoy

1828–1910

ON the estate of Yasnaya Polyana, which lies a hundred and thirty miles from Moscow, there is a grassy knoll surrounded by nine great oaks, and here, just over a century ago, four young brothers used to play. To climb the oaks and sit among the green boughs was their chief delight. One of these brothers was the great Tolstoy, and where he had played as a boy his body now rests. He has returned to the scenes of his childhood.

Indeed, one cannot get away from the conviction that Tolstoy's childhood had a profound influence on his whole life, for he lost his mother when he was two years old and his father when he was nine. The important early influence of parents, therefore, was lacking, and his training, for good or ill, was received from tutors, who, worthy though they may be, are incalculable. They may give to their charges the utmost care, according to their lights, but it is not to be expected that they can ever take the place of conscientious parents.

Tolstoy came of an old aristocratic family, and he was an affectionate, lively and intelligent boy, but he was also extremely introspective, he wept easily, and he was deeply dissatisfied with his character and looks. Indeed, he was not handsome, with his stiff dark hair, broad nose, thick lips, high cheekbones and small grey eyes. As he grew older he became somewhat arrogant and opinionated, yet he made the most strenuous efforts to be humble, and when he fell from grace he suffered intensely. On these occasions, poor child, he would pray to the soul of his dead mother for guidance. Yet although he was often unhappy, yet his capacity for living was immense; music enchanted him, and beauty, especially in nature, sent him into ecstacies.

It is, in fact, fascinating to watch the early opening of this flower of genius, for even as a very young boy he was thirsting for knowledge, eager to know the why and wherefore of everything, and fiercely ambitious. It is clear that he was vaguely conscious of great powers and was determined to keep abreast of modern thought. Rousseau's works he devoured with ardour, and he was so enamoured of the man that he wore his medallion portrait next his body, instead of the orthodox crucifix. The young Tolstoy became very sceptical about religion, too, at this time, a state of mind which led him, as he says, 'to the verge of insanity'. He imagined that besides himself nothing existed in the universe, and there were moments when, under the influence of this fixed idea, he would look rapidly round to one side, 'hoping to catch nothingness unawares'.

In the meantime he resolutely drew up a plan for disciplined work, a plan which we, at this distance of time, can only contemplate with awe and admiration. Here are the tasks he planned:

1. To study the whole course of the Law necessary to get my degree.
2. To study practical medicine, and to some extent its theory also.
3. To study French, Russian, German, English, Italian and Latin.
4. To study Agriculture, theoretically and practically.
5. To study History, Geography and Statistics.
6. To study Mathematics (the High School course.)
7. To write my (University) Thesis.
8. To reach the highest perfection I can in music and painting.
9. To write down rules (for my conduct).
10. To acquire some knowledge of the Natural Sciences, and
11. To write Essays on all the subjects I study.

He was also determined:

1. To fulfil what I set myself despite all obstacles.

LEO TOLSTOY

2. To fulfil well what I undertake.
3. Never to refer to a book for what I have forgotten, but always to try to recall it to mind myself.
4. Always to make my mind work with its utmost power.
5. Always to think and read aloud.
6. Not to be ashamed of telling people who interrupt me that they are hindering me, letting them first feel it, but (if they do not understand) telling them, with an apology.

That he achieved even one-tenth of this colossal programme we gravely doubt, but we know that eventually he entered Kazan University and matriculated in 1844. We know, too, that by the time he entered the army as a cadet he had become very conscious of his high birth and was much impressed by elegant manners, splendid clothes and wealth and rank. He saw active service in the Caucasus, eventually received his commission, and fought at Sevastopol, then finally he began to write his experiences as a soldier, a series of articles which were so excellent that they attracted the attention of the Tsar, who sent instructions to 'take care of the life of that young man'.

But Tolstoy was far from happy, as he was moody, boastful, irritable and difficult; he disliked army life, and despised most of his brother-officers. Also, there were times when he seemed to be possessed of a devil. Sometimes he would gamble for days, losing and winning alternately; then finally he would stake almost all that he possessed, even his estate. As a result, he was often heavily in debt. After these orgies he suffered agonies of remorse, and he swore that he would alter his life, but again and again he failed to keep his vows.

We read this part of his diary, in fact, with dismay, for if ever a young man needed the kindly guidance and advice of parents it was this young soldier. Debts, debauchery, ill-health, remorse; there is no end to it. Women—and gypsy singers in particular— were a torture to him, and as a result he came to feel that all women were evil and that sexual desire was a grievous sin. His passions, in fact, were so strong that sometimes his days and nights were a torment. Yet through all this he was vaguely conscious of some great purpose. 'For what am I destined?' he demanded. 'The future will reveal it.'

Such was the man who, when released from the army, went to live in the fabulous city of Petersburg, and took part in the fashionable round of high society. He travelled on the Continent, too, and here we catch a glimpse of him as a young man who was determined to attract attention. He would make social calls wearing a fur-trimmed overcoat and a glossy hat (placed carefully to one side of his curly dark-brown head), but the next day he would appear in the costume of a Spanish bandit. On another occasion he attended a smart At Home wearing tourist tweeds and wooden sabots!

But it was after his return to Russia that he began again to sow his wild oats, though with fits of passionate remorse and self-loathing, before finally settling down at Yasnaya Polyana, his country estate. Here, with the assistance of 309 male serfs he lived the life of a country squire, farming, breeding horses, hunting and shooting. He also took to himself a peasant mistress, by whom he had an illegitimate son.

Yet it is clear that this life did not satisfy him, and he was anxious to marry. He believed that marriage would solve all his problems, although it did not apparently occur to him to consider whether he could make a woman happy in marriage. The theory of the Middle Ages—that women were more or less chattels—was accepted as a matter of course, and in his courtship of a young girl he considered it his duty to give her plenty of advice. The young girl must have found it extremely difficult to please her critical admirer: 'She had her hair done up in a terrible fashion', he wrote in his diary, 'and wore a purple mantle, for *me*. I felt pained and ashamed and spent a sad day.' On one occasion, too, she wore a white dress with bare arms, and the arms, unfortunately, were not shapely, according to Tolstoy. Another sad day!

He was determined, however, to mould her to his pattern.

Please walk every day (he wrote) whatever the weather may

be . . . also wear your stays and put on your stockings yourself, and generally make improvements of that kind in yourself. Do not despair of becoming perfect. . . . Try, please, please, to plan the day's occupations in advance and check them off in the evening.

The lord and master is here revealed. 'Do not despair of becoming perfect', indeed. Did he for one moment consider how far he was from becoming perfect himself? Did he for one moment consider how he could possibly make a young girl happy in marriage, he with his deplorable passions and debaucheries, his strange, conflicting desires, his jealousy, his tears, protestations and remorses? It would seem from his diary that the thought did not occur to him. The courtship of this young girl, however, came to nothing.

But soon another young woman took his fancy; she was beautiful, intelligent, eighteen years of age and very much in love with Tolstoy. They were soon engaged, and then, just before their marriage—when there was barely time to withdraw, he insisted that she should read his diary, that frank document in which he had set down all his incredible follies and excesses. She did not want to read it—nothing could have been more painful—but he insisted, and she read it with the utmost horror.

Nevertheless the marriage took place, and she came to share his life at Yasnaya Polyana. She was a restless and highly-strung young girl, and Tolstoy was for most of his time completely absorbed in his writing. But he was also very passionate, possessive and jealous. There can be no doubt, however, that they were fairly happy, for she was extremely proud of him, she helped him with his literary work and with the peasant school which he had started. She also bore him many children. As for Tolstoy, those wonderful books, *War and Peace* and *Anna Karenina*, were written during the first ten years of his married life, and he was hailed as a magnificent writer.

But this life which appeared to be so full and interesting was merely so on the surface. Beneath the exterior of this remarkable author-landowner, with his hunting, shooting, fishing, gymnastics, guitar playing, etc., there was a volcano, ready at any moment to break out and shoot forth flames of fire. 'Why am I living? What is the purpose of life?' These questions began to hammer at him night and day, with maddening insistency. 'Why am I living? Why am I living?' It was an obsession, it was unbearable, for he could find no answer. Had no one ever asked this question before? Of course, perhaps since the world began, but with Tolstoy a question asked must be answered; there could be no compromise.

He was amazed indeed that he had lived for years surrounded by problems and evils which obviously cried out for urgent remedies. The whole world seemed to be a hideous mistake, a joke in the worst possible taste. It was in desperation, therefore, that Tolstoy turned to the Church, and with characteristic earnestness he visited monasteries, and talked for days with priests and monks. Yet there was little comfort there, for he was quite unable to accept the greater part of the Church's teaching; he believed only in the teaching of Christ.

It was, of course, impossible for him to hide his feelings from his family, as his state of mind was accompanied by intense depression. He wept often, longed to die, and wished to put an end to his life. He became afraid to go to his room in case he should hang himself—from a cord suspended there for gymnastic purposes. He also gave up shooting in case he should be tempted to turn the gun on himself.

At last he came to the conclusion that money was the root of all evil, that it was wrong to be rich, and that only the poor, who toiled with their hands, knew the true meaning of living. How he pitied the poor! 'My heart breaks with despair that we have all gone astray', he cried, and in his enthusiasm for this new idea he decided to renounce everything and give all that he possessed to the peasants. But the Countess—as well she might be—was horrified at the idea; she could not possibly agree. Did he not realise that he had a large family which must be educated and provided for? Did he not realise—brilliant man though he was

—that his first duty was to them? Yes, of course he realised it, and he was willing to hand all his property over to her. The Countess, however, replied with tears that she could not possibly accept the responsibility. They were his children too. Why should she have to guide them, arrange for their education and start them in life? It was too much, too much. She could not do it.

The scenes, tears, reproaches and hysterics, in fact which took place in the Tolstoy household would fill a book. But the great man was not to be moved. He was determined, at any rate, to live like a peasant, so he began to dress in rough labourer's clothes, and he insisted on cleaning his own room and lighting his own stove. The poor had done it for centuries. Why should not he? He also learnt to plough, dig, harrow, scythe and manure the land. He even tried to make his own shoes (alas, they did not fit!). Any suggestion of elegance, of course, was quite out of the question, and when he passed fine shops and theatres, or saw a well-laid table, or an immaculate turn-out of carriage, horses and coachman, he was deeply grieved. It seemed that the poor starved and died in garrets while the rich lived in idleness and luxury.

Two or three years passed in this mood, and then other ideas forced themselves upon him. There was his theory of non-resistance to evil, and his objection to conscription and war; there was his protest against the prison and exile system, and his refusal to do jury service. He also condemned all service in Governments or connected with churches, all forms of capitalism, or the owning of property, all commerce and professional medicine. Railways, too, were an abomination, and on principle he decided to walk. A journey from Moscow to Polyana Yasnaya, therefore —130 miles—was made on foot, sleeping in hovels on the way. Finally he became a vegetarian, gave up smoking and alcohol, and decided never to hunt again.

But the Countess was openly contemptuous of these new ideas, and some of her children agreed with her. The others, however, were influenced by their father and even wished to follow his example and live as peasants, a suggestion that angered the Countess almost beyond endurance. 'Counts you were born and

Counts you shall remain', she said firmly. It was, however, a struggle with forces that she could not control, and this and the ever-increasing burden of bearing children undermined her health, so that she too became hysterical, difficult and even suicidal. She knew not where to turn and was grieved beyond words that this great artist should have buried his genius and become a propagandist. She remembered how Turgenev, just before he died, had begged Tolstoy to return to his true literary activity.

Yet although Tolstoy had changed, his powerful literary genius had in no way diminished. He still wrote books, but with a purpose, and in 1886 he produced that great play *The Power of Darkness*. Three years later he wrote *The Kreutzer Sonata*, one of the strangest and most provocative books that has ever been written. How it shook Russia! And even those authors who could not agree with his idea were profoundly stirred by the superb skill with which he had written the book. The Church, of course, was angry, for in addition to this book he had also translated the Gospels, omitting everything he did not accept or believe. What was to be done with such a man? After due deliberation they could but denounce him as anti-Christ. But he was not in the least concerned, for his conscience was perfectly clear.

The Government also disapproved of his books, and newspaper men and editors were fined and even arrested for publishing his works. Even the Tsar was affected by this matter, for Tolstoy wrote long letters to him. 'Dear brother', he began, and there followed a great many suggestions and warnings, especially with regard to legal justice and the rights of the people.

Meanwhile, the house at Yasnaya Polyana had become almost a place of pilgrimage, and visitors arrived daily, demanding to see Tolstoy. They confessed to him and wept at his feet; they wanted help, money or advice. He would speak seriously to each one, but he could rarely advise them, as he himself was still wrestling in the dark. Then at last he came to a decision about his property, and in the year 1891 he divided it amongst his family. At the same time he renounced the copyright of his works and refused to accept money for anything he wrote. It was wrong, he decided, that a poor student or teacher might deprive himself of real necessities in order to buy his books. He wrote, however, many more books and pamphlets—on Religion, The Gospels, Patriotism, Art, 'The Slavery of our Times', etc. He was determined to reform the world, and his voice rang like a great bell through Russia. Under the spell of his words thousands of young men and women became his disciples and endeavoured to live according to his philosophy; colonies were founded, and rich young aristocrats renounced their wealth and went out into the desert. Yet the Holy Synod excommunicated him, his books were banned from public libraries, and sermons were preached against him all over the world. He was even threatened with murder, but none of these things influenced him in the least; he sought the truth and was ready to lay down his life for it.

Tolstoy's views, however, were not original; they had all been expounded before, but never by such a supreme artist. It was the tremendous power and ardour of his writing which gave him such a huge audience. Yet eventually it was this very ardour which alienated him from many of his friends, estranged him from his wife, and divided his own children against him.

As the tragedy of Tolstoy's end draws near the part played by one of his most earnest disciples, V. G. Chertkov, becomes increasingly significant. This man obtained a great influence over Tolstoy —who was quite convinced of his sincerity, but the Countess neither liked nor trusted Chertkov, and there are good reasons for thinking she was right. In the end he certainly caused serious dissension in the family, for he drew up a will which was, in effect, extremely beneficial to himself. Unknown to the Countess, the will was smuggled into the house and Tolstoy was induced to sign it. Chertkov also became possessed of certain of Tolstoy's private diaries, a fact which was very distressing to the Countess, as they revealed much in their married life which she deplored and regretted. She, poor wretched woman, had become neurasthenic, and although Tolstoy declared that he still loved her, she knew that Chertkov had a far greater influence. Her worries were increased, also, by the fact that her children were painfully divided in their sympathies.

Quarrels and scenes became more and more frequent, and Tolstoy was harassed on every side. 'They tear me to pieces', he declared miserably.

Finally, one evening he found his wife searching amongst his papers, and he felt that life at Yasnaya Polyana had become unbearable. He had for a long time submitted to conditions which were extremely painful to him, he was over eighty, ill and weary, and his one idea was to hide himself somewhere. The following morning, therefore (the date was the 28th October, 1910) he left the house. He had no plans, he merely wished to get away. But the weather was cold, and on the train journey he caught a chill. Finally he was obliged to rest at the station-master's house at Astapovo, where some of his children and Chertkov joined him. He realised that he had not long to live and expressed concern for his wife, yet was afraid that if they met a painful scene would ensue. When the Countess did arrive at Astapovo she was refused admission to the sick-room, and not until Tolstoy was unconscious and actually dying was she allowed to see him. It was a sad ending to a long married life. But how unhappy she had been! 'Let no one raise a hand against me', she wrote in her diary, 'for I have suffered terribly.'

Tolstoy met his death quite calmly, and as he would have wished, he spent his last moments in a simple cottage. But there was little simplicity connected with his death, for five doctors were in attendance, the station-master had been turned out of his house to make room for visitors, the village was thronged with press photographers, journalists, government officials and policemen, etc. In fact, so large was the crowd that they had to be accommodated in empty railway carriages. His burial, too, caused far more disturbance than he would have wished, for although the Holy Synod forbade memorial services to be held in the churches, nevertheless the private theatres were closed, the newspapers appeared with black borders, and Petersburg University suspended lectures for the day.

Such are the bare facts of Tolstoy's life, but from these facts the whole psychology of the man can be laid bare. And one fact stands out above all others—Tolstoy was born an artist; the extreme sensitiveness, the strong emotions, the marvellous faculty of observation, the love of beauty, the idealism; here were all the qualities of a great author, But he came to maturity at a time when immense changes were taking place in Russia. The peasants were being emancipated and the public conscience was steadily awakening. There was tremendous unrest everywhere, for in no country in the world was there so much injustice and repression, or so much disparity between the rich and the poor. Tolstoy, with his marvellous sensitiveness, was caught by the movement like a tidal wave. He did not believe in violence, but someone must rouse the people. And he had a voice that could roll and echo like thunder. He had courage, too, and a burning sincerity. So who else should speak for Russia?

He spoke, and the world listened. But in his preoccupation with social problems Art was cast aside,—a serious loss indeed to posterity. Yet that Tolstoy achieved much for Russia cannot be denied, and he was right, of course, to criticise the self-complacency of the privileged classes. Nevertheless it is a fact that he was at the height of his creative powers when his 'conversion' took place, and when he ceased to be a literary artist. Great and immortal works might still have issued from his pen, books which might have been a perpetual inspiration to the highest minds for centuries. We cannot, indeed, tell how great is the loss to the world. And in their place are pamphlets, sermons, treatises, all extremely interesting because they are presented by a great author, but all controversial and therefore of doubtful value. The questions of chastity, of non-resistance to evil, and of property, for instance, can never be solved by one answer. It must be admitted, too, that as Tolstoy over-simplified his problems, so are his remedies impracticable. In a highly civilized society they simply would not work, and would certainly create greater problems. But the artist, of course, is not a single-minded man. He writes out of his inner conflicts, and although he is poignantly aware of the dilemmas of human beings he can rarely tell us what to do; he can only tell us what we are.

So Tolstoy erred where many others have erred before him. He saw great evils, and in his impatience and anger he snatched at simple remedies, remedies which have always failed when put to the test. For instance, none of the colonies or groups founded by his disciples in Russia or elsewhere were successful, or able to hold to his principles. In the first place, the land needed for such colonies could not be bought without the assistance of lawyers, surveyors and landowners, of whom Tolstoy entirely disapproved. His disciples did not agree, either, with criminal or civil laws, as they considered that men and women should be guided only by their own consciences. Misunderstandings in these colonies were therefore bound to arise, for each man's conscience told him something different, and these well-meaning but misguided people spent endless time and energy in arguing and quarrelling; so that co-operation in the end became impossible.

Yet we must be grateful for the wonderful books Tolstoy did produce, especially for *War and Peace*, which can only be described as a marvellous work of art. For here, on an immense stage, we are shown a panoramic vision of great significance; it is vivid, intensely stirring, and crowded with life. We are shown the salons of Petersburg, and the camps of war, but we see also how one generation replaces the next, how the torch of life is handed on, ever with new enthusiasm. It is a magnificent book, in which every scene stands out with remarkable beauty, and these characters are so real that were we suddenly transported to Russia we feel that we should recognise the very houses and streets; the very beggars would have a familiar look.

What a wealth of poetry there is, too, in his *Childhood*, a book that contains all the poignancy of youth—the deep yearning, the exquisite happiness, the wild hopes, the beautiful faith and wonder at this strange world! Every line of this book is steeped in the very scent of Russia. Indeed, when Tolstoy writes of a spring day one can smell the lilacs, and feel the warm rain on one's face; one can hear the birds singing in the orchard and see the apple-blossom drifting to the ground. Such is Tolstoy's power, for his story-telling is different from any other story-telling in the world; it is more alive, intense, true.

As for Tolstoy himself, he stands out from the canvas with such strength and vividness that we are never tired of gazing on that portrait. Whether he is galloping past wearing his Cossack cloak, or scything the corn, or hunting with his borzois, or sitting at his window playing a guitar and singing a gypsy love song, or playing chess, or skating, or ploughing, or swinging on his parallel bars, or dancing at a Petersburg ball, there is something so vital about him that it is almost godlike. His critics may remind us of his follies, his egotism, his vices, his vanity and his inconsistencies, but we remember only his passionate sincerity, his wonderful gaiety, his courage, his tenderness, his enthusiasm. We remember how at the age of sixty-three he and his wife worked unceasingly amongst the starving peasants; they opened communal kitchens and fed thousands of people, and they continued this work for two years, finally also assisting the peasants to re-establish themselves. 'Tolstoy, ah Tolstoy!' said Tchehov. 'He is not a man, but a superman, a Jupiter.' We remember, too, how fine Tolstoy's intentions were and that he did his utmost to live up to his creed. If sometimes he did not succeed he is merely the more human.

Anton Tchehov

1860–1904

IN the very early years of the twentieth century a visitor to the seaside town of Yalta, in Russia, might have observed, sitting on the seafront, a tall, handsome man with a dark, pointed beard and twinkling humorous eyes. He would watch the passers-by for a time, and then, with slow deliberation, stroll back to an elegant, white, balconied house, not so far away. It was a house of rather unusual design, with a watch-tower, and it had been built specially for the distinguished author, Anton Pavlovitch Tchehov, who had been ordered by his doctor to live in Yalta during the winter months, for his health.

Everyone in Yalta knew Tchehov by sight, and he was such a celebrity that young aspiring authors would hang about his house for hours, trying to catch a glimpse of him. They would even write to him, enclosing their huge untidy manuscripts, and begging for advice and criticism. Young girls, too, who had heard so much of the author's charm and fame, would stand at the gate, peering into the garden. And sometimes they were fortunate enough to see him sitting under a flowering tree, reading. He was, indeed, very handsome. And occasionally, seated beside him would be a lovely red-haired woman, with a brilliant smile and dimples; she was the gayest, most delightful creature, always laughing, always showing her beautiful teeth. This was Tchehov's actress wife, Olga Knipper, famous throughout Russia as a talented member of the Moscow Art Theatre Company.

Olga Knipper, however, came very rarely, for she was generally with her Theatre Company in Moscow, or in Petersburg, or on tour. But occasionally the Moscow Art Theatre Company would

ANTON TCHEHOV

come to Yalta for a week or so; they would act Tchehov's plays, and the town would become almost a festival of flowers. Everyone in Yalta adored Tchehov, for his kindness and generosity were proverbial, and he was so gentle, modest and unassuming. Those who knew him said that he was also a most amusing man, with a delightful sense of humour. When the Moscow Art Theatre Company arrived in Yalta, there were the gayest parties up at the white house; one could hear the merry laughter even as one walked past the gates. And what a host of celebrities gathered in that garden! The beautifully dressed actresses walking on the lawns and under the trees were a joy to see.

It was said that Tchehov had made a fortune out of his books, but this was not so; he merely made a comfortable livelihood. And how he had slaved for it! Night and day, for years, never sparing himself, he had worked at his craft. For many years, too, he had worked in the country amongst the peasants as a doctor, but at the same time he had written many wonderful books. His life story was a splendid example to aspiring authors, for although there can be no doubt that he was born with the potentialities of genius, his theory was that work mattered most. 'An author must work every day', he said, 'without fail.' He believed that if a man was talented he should be willing to sacrifice health, love, and even life itself for that great gift. There was no short cut to the fulfilment of genius; every moment was precious.

Indeed, looking back on his own life he could barely remember a day on which he had been able to take his ease. His had been a life of incessant work, and although the act of creation was a joy, yet how an author's profession cut him off from the world! And how exhausting it was! For one was essentially a perfectionist, and the urge to realise one's high ideal was incessant; it drove one on, day and night; one could never get away from it. So, almost before he had realised what had happened, his youth was gone, his health was impaired, and the sparkle of life had departed.

All this, however, must be hidden, except to one's most intimate friends; one must give no sign that life had lost its flavour, but one must make jokes, tease one's youthful admirers and continue to laugh heartily. One must be careful, too, about looks and clothes, for an actress wife had eyes like a hawk; she who was much admired and sought after liked her husband to be not only famous and handsome, but elegant. She insisted that he changed his suit every day, etc. And he who adored the very rings on her fingers, who feverishly counted the days between her visits, could do no other than comply. He had been married for only a few years, yet she was the very reason for his existence, the brilliant light round which he fluttered like a hapless moth. When they were apart he merely existed; he did not live. 'Ah, darling, darling', he wrote . . . 'Without you I am good for nothing.' Yet he never begrudged her her parties and gaiety. 'Be well, merry, happy', he said. 'I bless you, my joy, my little beetle.'

It was when the nineteenth century had still some forty years to run that Anton Tchehov had first opened his eyes to the world in a poor room above a small grocer's shop in Taganrog; and the date of Anton's birth was significant, for the emancipation of the serfs was soon to take place and Tchehov's father had himself started life as a serf, a fact which was hard to forget. For how difficult it was for a man to squeeze the slave out of himself; the old subservient attitude was inbred. Anton's father, therefore, bowed low always to his superiors, flopped to the ground before a bishop, crossed himself twenty times a day, and beat his children as he himself had been beaten. He had been reared in the strictest orthodox faith, and he was choirmaster at the Taganrog Church, so his children were trained to sing in the choir, to assist at the altar, to ring the church bells, etc. And if these duties were not performed satisfactorily the boys were thrashed. The days were a constant succession of services, processions, and practices, and every night his children were made to practise under his strict direction, often until midnight. Sometimes they were almost too tired to creep up to bed. But the stern choirmaster had no mercy on them. 'The boy chanters at Mount Athos sing for nights on end', he said, 'and I myself have sung from my early childhood. To work for God is never harmful.'

These incessant practices and church services, however, were torture to Anton, and the thrashings which accompanied any lack of enthusiasm were degrading and humiliating. He was a merry and humorous boy, but how he longed to have time to read, to be alone a little, just in order to think! Why was he made, in every spare moment, to serve in the shop? How he loathed the petty dishonesties with false weight which his father insisted upon! 'I had no childhood', he declared later.

Indeed, at the age of sixteen he was suddenly thrown entirely upon his own resources, for his father went bankrupt, the house and furniture were sold by auction, and the whole family departed to Moscow. Anton, with admirable self-reliance, decided to stay in Taganrog until he had matriculated at the High School, and to earn his own living by tutoring. Tutoring was extremely badly paid, but what other work was open to him? Day after day, therefore, in his threadbare coat and worn shoes, he would tramp through the snow from one pupil to another. Then at night, utterly weary, he was obliged to study for his own examinations. For three years this was his life, and often he was obliged to go hungry. His loneliness and despair, too, cannot be measured, yet he could not and would not complain, for his people were having a bitter struggle against poverty and were quite unable to assist him.

By the time he had matriculated, at the age of nineteen, however, and had joined the family in Moscow, he had developed into a handsome, self-reliant and highly intelligent youth. He had no capital, no influence and no prospects, but he was determined to become a medical student at Moscow University and at the same time to earn a living as a journalist and author. Tutoring, also, added to his earnings.

He soon discovered, however, that he was expected to be the main support of his family and also to contribute largely towards the education of his younger brothers and sister. In addition to his medical studies, therefore, he wrote incessantly, night and day, working always at great speed and under the most difficult conditions, as there was neither peace nor privacy in that large family. They were all affectionate and devoted, but noisy, irresponsible and consistently impecunious. Nevertheless, most of the stories he wrote at this time were humorous in character. Such was the unquenchable gaiety of this remarkable youth.

When finally he had obtained his medical degree one might have prophesied for this brilliant young man a fine future as a doctor, but he had already made a name as an author and eventually he was awarded the Pushkin prize (500 roubles). 'They regale me with food and drink like a General at a wedding', he said, but he bore his success with admirable modesty and declared that he had had a terrific run of luck. 'I feel ashamed of the public which runs after lap-dogs simply because it fails to notice elephants . . . and I am deeply convinced that not a soul will know me when I begin to write in earnest', he said.

Thus did his genius blossom, but even as it came to fruition the tone of his stories changed. How, indeed, could it be otherwise, when Russia was seething with urgent problems, and only authors, under the cloak of fiction, were allowed to speak? It was clear that writing must be regarded as a serious social task, for the printed word could have immense influence; possibly the fate of Russia depended upon its authors. Tchehov was no revolutionary, however; he did not believe that it was essential to destroy the past in order to build anew. What was needed was long and patient endeavour. The emancipation of the serfs had been achieved, and surely in time other reforms would come! The Tsar was inflexible; his will was law. The Military and Government officials, too, were ruthless in their administration. Free speech was impossible, discussion of any political problem was strictly forbidden, and thousands of young men, professors and students had been sent to Siberia merely for debating questions which in England would have been perfectly legal. This was the Russia in which Tchehov had grown up, and even authors had to write with the greatest caution. Tchehov knew, in fact, that spies watched and followed him wherever he went.

Meanwhile, he continued steadily with his work. He would begin in the early hours of the morning, and sometimes when dawn broke over the city he was still at his desk, writing by candle-light. The willing horse was taken for granted, and few of his friends or relatives realised what it cost him to maintain this prodigious effort. He confessed to a friend that a whole organisation rested upon his shoulders, which would collapse if he had not kept up his output. He had a mother and sister, and younger brothers still at the University; there was an artist brother who was idle, drunken and almost worthless; all these people relied on him, and in utter selflessness he had shouldered the burden. But for this effort he was already paying the price, as sometimes he was utterly exhausted and had already shown signs of tuberculosis. The late nights, the lack of rest, the drain on his energy and the continual family anxieties were taking their toll. He had inherited a strong constitution from his peasant forebears, but there was a limit even to his endurance.

Yet there were diversions, for in summer he would rent for himself and his family a small lodge in the country. Fishing was one of his few relaxations, and when the river ran at his feet and his line floated serenely on the water there was not a happier man in Russia. During these summer vacations he also did a certain amount of medical work, particularly amongst the peasants, for doctors were extremely scarce. He was rarely paid anything for his services, but the work brought its own reward; the poor peasants were so deeply grateful. It is true that their squalor and drunken habits were deplorable, yet there was something infinitely touching about their courage, piety and simple philosophy. They met death unflinchingly, utterly resigned to the will of God.

Yes, the peasants were extremely interesting to write about. Nor was there any lack of material in other walks of life—in the Law Courts, in the Monasteries, in country inns and in hospitals. Life, to this young author, was an enthralling and fascinating panorama, inexhaustible in its interest. But as Tchehov's fame grew, so did the 'insufferable crowd of visitors'. They invaded his privacy, wasted his time, thrust their manuscripts upon him, and even went so far as to lecture him on his duty as an author. Sometimes for days he had not a moment's peace. Women admirers, too, were extremely embarrassing; there were women who believed that he wished to marry them, yet he had never given them the slightest encouragement. He could not possibly marry; his responsibilities were far too great. His attempts to write plays, too, proved almost heartbreaking. He loved the theatre, but his first play had caused an uproar, and his second play had been a dismal failure, a failure that had shaken him profoundly. It was inevitable that he should be sensitive about his work, for these plays were written with his heart's blood; he could not take them lightly.

It was at this time, therefore, that Tchehov decided to desert literature for a time and devote himself to some serious altruistic work. There was one terrible problem which he was determined to assist—the cruel matter of penal settlement in Russia. Men had been driven in chains for thousands of miles in Siberia, and had worked there for years under the most appalling conditions. Hundreds had been destroyed there, body and soul, and it seemed that no one cared. Tchehov was determined to visit the convict island of Sahalin, to make a thorough investigation, and then by publishing the facts draw attention to the whole question of exile. His journey, however, proved a most difficult one, as the Trans-Siberian railway did not then exist and he was forced to drive across Siberia with horses, day and night, in an open chaise, for nearly three thousand miles. He encountered storms, floods and torrential rain.

Sahalin was a fearful revelation, a living hell, but he made a complete tour of the island, interviewed every one of the ten thousand convicts and made a detailed census. It was exhausting and depressing work, yet he stayed there for three months, and on his return wrote many articles and a book on the subject, articles which certainly contributed to the reform which came later. The cost of this trip was borne entirely by himself, and at a time when his family were still partly dependent on him. On his return, therefore, he was obliged to work harder than ever, writing day and night.

It was in 1892, on the urgent advice of his doctors, that Tchehov bought a small estate in the country, and settled there with his family. He knew nothing of farming, but he bought books on the subject and worked accordingly. As newcomers to country life and ways the Tchehovs were flagrantly cheated and robbed by the peasants, yet in time they were accepted, and Tchehov's work as a doctor made him much beloved. There was however little peace for this great-hearted young man, for Russia was constantly beset by troubles, and Tchehov was always asked to assist. There were serious famines and epidemics of cholera. Tchehov worked nobly for months on schemes of famine relief, and for the cholera epidemic he organised the erection, staffing and equipment of temporary hospitals, and finally took charge of a large district covering twenty-five villages. There were no funds available for this work, so he himself drove round the countryside collecting money. Later, too, he built schools (largely at his own expense), a fire-station, and a belfry for the church; he also constructed new roads and assisted in the erection of a permanent hospital. His literary work, of course, never ceased, and his medical work amongst the peasants went on continually—until, in fact, his strength utterly gave out. Finally he had a serious haemorrhage of the lungs and was in hospital in Moscow for some weeks.

However, the years passed, and with them came a measure of peace. When the estate in Melihovo was eventually sold he went to live in Yalta, and it was there that he married his lovely wife, who brought him, indeed, much happiness. The storm-tossed boat had come into harbour at last. It is true that he called Yalta 'that devil's island', and that often he felt wretchedly isolated so far from Moscow. But visits to the Continent, where he sometimes spent the winter, were some consolation. And there was always work. When his health was good, writing was a joy. Besides, there was no longer any urgency for his work.

Tchehov died in the year 1904, in Germany, where he had gone with his wife for a cure, And he died, as he had lived, with immense courage, for within a few hours of his death he merrily related an amusing story to his wife. But his work was finished; no man in Russia had ever fulfilled his task more faithfully. The talent which he had inherited he had used to the full, not for his own glory and aggrandisement but for his fellow-men.

Yet as we consider this great author, we are bound to ask ourselves how he and his contemporaries came to write so magnificently, what it was that made them see so clearly and feel so deeply. The answer lies, surely, in their utter lack of self-consciousness. The culture of Russia was of such recent growth that it had not had time to crush their vitality, their natural sympathies, their simplicity. They could feel, not with the mind alone, but with the heart. Life for them, in fact, still consisted of fundamentals; the fundamentals had not yet got mixed up with the inessentials. For indeed, when one has neither silver teapots nor jewellery, nor fine books, nor tapestries to worry about, there is time to notice that one's wife is wretched or ill, that one's children are in love, that the dog needs water. There is time to notice the beauty of the earth, the brightness of the stars at night, the grace of the changing seasons. And not only is there time, but the true sense of values has not been lost.

But we are principally concerned now with Tchehov. Was his great claim to authorship merely a clever gift, the result of infinite care and pains? No, indeed, it was his rare nobility of soul which set the stamp upon his work. There was no public school to instil into him the principles of honour and integrity; there was no fine house hung with elegant pictures to foster in him the love of art and beauty. There was nothing but a peasant father and mother, wretched poverty, grinding work and a poor miserable grocer's shop for his environment. But that great soul triumphed over all these obstacles. No aristocrat in Russia had finer susceptibilities or more exquisite taste. No nobleman had a higher sense of honour or a greater sense of duty. Life was a precious gift which was meant to be noble.

In reading his stories, too, we realise that here is an author without bias or prejudice; he is neither indifferent, nor indignant, nor cynical nor bitter. There is no evidence, either, of any prudishness or narrow superstition, or harsh asceticism. And—heaven be praised—there are no literary tricks. Tchehov makes no attempt to accuse, to judge, or to condemn. Yet what a marvellous power of selection is here, and what artistry! His characters stand out with amazing reality; we know the background of their whole lives, and the sound of their voices; we laugh and cry with them. For this is Russian literature, and there is nothing quite like it in the world. It is so strong, and moving and beautiful, even after translation, that our own literature looks crude and superficial in comparison.

Yet if these people are real, their surroundings are equally so. Without any effort on our part we can hear the bells of Moscow ringing and see the streets piled high with snow. The trees are feathered with frost, the houses are fringed with icicles; bells jingle as the sleighs glide past, and elegant young women in fur coats and caps rustle into the smart restaurants. . . . A hungry child stands gazing into a confectioner's window, a beggar in filthy rags leans against a church door. . . . Then suddenly we are in a peasant village on a summer's evening; the sun is sinking behind the flowering rye and shining on the glittering cross that belongs to every Russian church. The peasants are sitting outside their log huts munching sunflower seeds; the rosy children, with their hair falling about their faces, tumble in the dust or swing lazily on the broken fences. . . . It is a world which we seem to know intimately.

As for Tchehov himself, inevitably we remember many things about him—that he loved the sound of church bells, that he kept a couple of tame cranes in his courtyard, that he adored flowers, and elegance, and pictures, that he went into raptures about sunsets and the scent of newmown hay. We remember that he hated hypocrisy and humbug, and disliked 'serious' conversations with pretentious intellectuals. Beauty was one of his gods, and he declared that 'the sense of beauty in man knows no bounds'. That is why, wherever he went, he created a beautiful garden. Peace be to his ashes.

Index

211

INDEX

JOHNSON, Samuel: manners and appearance, 58–59; fame and social success, 59–60; friendship with Mrs. Thrale, 60; early life, work and marriage, 61; opens school, *Dictionary*, 61; contacts with royalty, forms men's club, 62; tours Scotland with Boswell, 63; Mrs. Thrale's second marriage and end of friendship with, 63–64; *The Lives of the Poets*, 65; disposal of library, tributes to, 65–66
JOHNSON, Mrs., 61

LAMB, Charles: 104, 112; education, 115–116; visits to Blakeswear, 116; temporary loss of reason, and illness of sister, 117; literary gatherings, appearance and peculiarities, 117–118; his Essays, 119; Islington, 120; Oxford and Cambridge, and visits to Coleridge, 121; qualities as an essayist, 122; love affairs, 122; characteristics, 123–124, 135, 136, 140, 146, 152
LAMB, Mary, 117, 118, 120, 121, 140

MILL, John Stuart, 161
MONTAIGNE, Michel de: 1; works on famous *Essays*, 2–3; appearance, characteristics, and life in his château, 3–5; publication and success of *Essays*, 5–6; friendship with La Boetie, 7, 8

PEPYS, Samuel: the diarist, 27, 31; early married life, 53–54; visits Holland to bring back Charles II, character, 54–55; life in London and clothes, 55; the *Diary*, 55–57; courage during Plague of London, 57; kindness of, 57

RALEIGH, Sir Walter: appearance and abilities, 10; Queen's favourite, 10; Durham House, 11; M.P., designs ships and plans fortifications, finances Colonisation expeditions, 11; his poetry, 12; attachment to Elizabeth Throgmorton, incurs Queen's displeasure, and sent to Tower, 12; Sherborne, 13; released from prison, and debarred from Court, 13; expedition to Guiana and successful action against Cadiz, 13; restored to favour, 13; implicated in plot against King, trial of, reprieved and sent to Tower, 14; released, 15; plans expedition, and failure of, 16; son's death, 16; betrayal of, and arrest at Plymouth, 16; warrant issued for death sentence, execution, 17; characteristics, 18; *History of the World*, 19
REYNOLDS, Sir Joshua, 62

SHELLEY, Percy Bysshe: generosity to Leigh Hunt, 139–140, 141; tragic death of, 142–143
SOUTHEY, Robert, 107, 108, 111, 133, 161

TAYLOR, Dr. Jeremy, 29
TCHEHOV, Anton: appearance and character, 200–201; plays produced at Yalta, 201; early days in Taganrog, and tutoring, 203; medical student at Moscow, and awarded Pushkin Prize, 203–204; hobbies, 205; love of the theatre, 206; Sahalin, 206; work as doctor, 207; married life, 207; claim to authorship, 207–209
THRALE, Mrs., 60, 63, 64, 66
TOLSTOY, Count Leo: 174; character and appearance, and influence of childhood in later life, 187; Sevastopol, 189; life in Petersburg, 190; marriage, 191; *War and Peace* and *Anna Karenina*, 191; turns to the Church, 192; life as a peasant, 193; literary genius, 194; pilgrimage to Yasnaya Polyana, 194–195; influence of Chertkov, 195; death of, and Holy Synod forbids memorial services, 196; achievements for Russia, 197, 198, 199